MASTERPIECES OF MODERN BRITISH AND IRISH DRAMA

Recent titles in
Greenwood Introduces Literary Masterpieces

Masterpieces of French Literature
Marilyn S. Severson

Masterpieces of 20th-Century American Drama
Susan C.W. Abbotson

MASTERPIECES OF MODERN BRITISH AND IRISH DRAMA

Sanford Sternlicht

Greenwood Introduces Literary Masterpieces

GREENWOOD PRESS
Westport, Connecticut • London

Library of Congress Cataloging-in-Publication Data

Sternlicht, Sanford V.
   Masterpieces of modern British and Irish drama / Sanford Sternlicht.
      p. cm. — (Greenwood introduces literary masterpieces, ISSN 1545–6285)
   Includes bibliographical references and index.
   ISBN 0–313–33323–8 (alk. paper)
   1. English drama—20th century—History and criticism. 2. English drama—Irish authors—
History and criticism. I. Title. II. Series.
PR736.S735 2005
822'.91099417—dc22   2005014518

British Library Cataloguing in Publication Data is available.

Library of Congress Catalog Card Number: 2005014518
ISBN: 0–313–33323–8
ISSN: 1545–6285

First published in 2005

Greenwood Press, 88 Post Road West, Westport, CT 06881
An imprint of Greenwood Publishing Group, Inc.
www.greenwood.com

Printed in the United States of America

The paper used in this book complies with the
Permanent Paper Standard issued by the National
Information Standards Organization (Z39.48–1984).

10 9 8 7 6 5 4 3 2 1

Contents

Acknowledgments

My thanks to Aaron Metosky, my research assistant, and Brian Calhoun-Bryant of Syracuse University's College of Arts and Sciences' Computing Services.

I especially thank my partner, Mary Beth Hinton, Syracuse University Library communications manager, for editorial assistance and patient reading of the manuscript of this book.

Introduction

TWO CULTURES HISTORICALLY ENTWINED

Modern British and Irish dramatic traditions are inextricably entwined because of the English language, the long British occupation of Ireland, and the ease of crossing from one island to the other by water. From the middle of the seventeenth century to the present time, Irish and English playwrights have worked both sides of the Irish Sea to the benefit of London and Dublin theater. London, being far larger and more important politically, benefited more because Irish writers were drawn to the capital of the British Empire for financial reasons and the lure of English society. Consequently, their plays were almost always performed first in London until the establishment of the Irish National Theatre Society in 1903 and the opening of the Abbey Theatre in Dublin in 1904. With the establishment of a national theater devoted to the production of plays on Irish themes by Irish writers, Irish drama began a century of significant contribution to English language and world drama. Britain would not have a national theater until the National Theatre Board was set up in 1962. However, the National Theatre did not begin to move into its present venue on the South Bank of the Thames until 1976. It became the Royal National Theatre in 1988.

The greatest Restoration playwright, William Congreve (1670–1769), was brought to Ireland from England at the age of four and was educated with Jonathan Swift at Kilkenny School and Trinity College, Dublin, prior to enrolling in Oxford. His masterpiece, the comedy *The Way of the World* (1700), is considered the finest play of the Restoration period. All his life, Congreve was taken for an Irishman because of his accent.

George Farquhar (1678–1707) was born in Derry and educated at Trinity College, Dublin. His comedies *The Recruiting Officer* (1706) and *The Beaux' Stratagem* (1707) held the stage for a hundred years. Dublin born Arthur Murphy (1727–1805) wrote successful tragedies and comedies for the English stage. Oliver Goldsmith (1728–1774) came from Pallas, County Longford, in the Irish Midlands, to Trinity College, Dublin, and then went on to London. His comedy *She Stoops to Conquer* (1773) is one of the comic masterpieces of eighteenth-century drama.

Richard Brinsley Sheridan (1751–1816), Dublin-born son of Thomas Sheridan, the manager of Dublin's Smock Alley Theatre, wrote the brilliant satiric comedy *School for Scandal* (1777). The prolific Dion Boucicault (1822–1890), Dublin-born playwright, entertained London, New York, and Dublin audiences with his spectacular melodramas that paved the way for the late twentieth-century musical extravaganzas like *Les Miserables* and *The Lion King*. His first play, the comedy *London Assurance* (1841), established his reputation as a playwright. His three Irish plays, *The Colleen Bawn* (1860), *Arrah na Pogue* (1864), and *The Shaughraum* (1874), are still performed in Ireland and America.

In the twentieth century, a stream of Irish playwrights, generally beginning their careers in Dublin, informed and enriched the English stage. Outstanding among them are William Butler Yeats (1865–1939), John Millington Synge (1871–1909), Sean O'Casey (1880–1964), Brian Friel (b. 1921), Marina Carr (b. 1964), and Martin McDonagh (b. 1971).

The influence of County Dublin–born and Trinity College–educated Samuel Beckett (1906–1989) on world drama is profound. *Waiting for Godot*, the first play in the Theater of the Absurd—existentialist tragicomedy implying that absurd life must be portrayed absurdly—is arguably the greatest play of the twentieth century.

In the nineteenth century, London actor-managers controlled the production of plays. Stars like Henry Irving commissioned plays that had fat roles for them. A resident company provided the necessary support for the lead actor, while playwrights were paid a fixed sum for their scripts, and all box office receipts went to the managers. Only a few bankable writers like Dion Boucicault, the master of the melodrama, could demand and receive percentages of the take. Thus, British theater languished in melodramas and revivals of Shakespeare.

Although the playwright Thomas William Robertson (1829–1871) introduced realism on the British stage with dramas like *Caste* in 1867, it was not until the work of two playwrights, Henry Arthur Jones (1852–1929) and Arthur Wing Pinero (1855–1934), that realism took hold. Jones and Pinero were even more under the influence of continental realism and naturalism when they and their followers, including George Bernard Shaw (1856–1950), began to liberate their craft by writing plays that were serious social dramas and witty comedies with believable characters.

Most significantly, just as the Norwegian Henrik Ibsen's (1828–1906) new social problem plays were being talked about in Britain, Pinero's *The Profligate* (1889) brought social drama to the British theater. Pinero's most influential play, *The Second Mrs. Tanqueray* (1893), focused on the much debated question of whether a "fallen woman" can ever be redeemed in polite society and whether a man's earlier sexual transgressions were as wrong and debilitating as a woman's. This theme reflected a major social issue of the day: the limited legal rights of women.

Although he started his playwriting career in 1882 with a very popular melodrama, *The Silver King*, Henry Arthur Jones (1851–1929) came to be regarded as a writer of serious plays on serious themes in the forefront of socially relevant drama. He, like Pinero, attacked the double standard, but Jones also took on religious hypocrisy in *Saints and Sinners* (1884), and in many of his dramas he made clear that he thought right and wrong are neither obvious nor clearly discernable in real life.

At the end of the nineteenth century, what was called The New Drama gave birth to modern British and Irish drama. The movement lasted from 1892 to 1914. It began with Shaw's *Widowers' Houses* in 1892 and reached its apex in Harley Granville-Barker's (1877–1946) and J.E. Vedrenne's (1867–1930) tenure as producers at the Royal Court Theatre from 1904 to 1907.

Early modern British drama also inherited the concept of the well-made play from the nineteenth century. Originating in French drama, the well-made play—a term that in the mid-twentieth century was used in derision—is a formulaic play in which plot takes precedence over characterization. In addition, action focuses on surprise and suspense, as the hero's fortune rises and falls and rises again. The hero usually has a chief adversary who is defeated in the end. Misunderstandings between a hero or heroine or between a parent and a child—resolved, of course, before the final curtain—also helped propel this plot-driven, carefully structured, and very popular dramatic form.

Modern Drama

Modern drama is international. It had its origins in the European intellectual, aesthetic, and cultural movement now called modernism. Modern drama's staple mode is realism, which in its extreme form is referred to as naturalism. The dramatic tenets of realism and naturalism include the integration of character with environment as well as motivated action that permits the exploration of political or social dynamics. Modernism both reflects and critiques the social and technological changes of the twentieth century.

Because of the plays of Henrik Ibsen, modernism came earlier to the drama than to art, literature, music, and dance, whose modernistic forms were conceived in the first quarter of the twentieth century. Ibsen's seminal and most provocative drama is *The Doll's House* (1878), in which a middle-class wife is treated like a loveable but brainless pet by her patriarchal husband. When, in a family crisis, she is subjected to vicious verbal abuse by her selfish and ungrateful husband, she realizes that she has had no life of her own and that she cannot love a man who could never truly respect her as a person. In an ending that shocked the theatergoing public of the Western world, Nora, the wife, walks out on her husband and children in order to gain self-respect and seek a new life for herself. With that play and others, Ibsen created social drama or thesis drama in which contemporary societal problems, such as venereal disease (*Ghosts* in 1882), or the rapaciousness of community leaders who place profit above public safety (*An Enemy of the People* in 1882) are highlighted for public view, debate, and instruction.

As the new mode spread throughout the European continent and on to Britain and Ireland, social drama irrevocably changed world drama. In Sweden, August Strindberg (1849–1912) focused on dimensions of the eternal war between the sexes in searing realistic dramas like *The Father* (1887) and *Miss Julie* (1889). With Strindberg and other modern playwrights, European critics and intelligentsia later found evidence of and support for their new fascination with the nascent psychoanalytic theories of Sigmund Freud (1856–1939).

But most important for us, it was George Bernard Shaw who brought modern drama to the British and subsequently the Irish stage.

Historical Background: 1899 to 2004

The twentieth century began early for Britain and Ireland. In 1899, Britain decided to add the Boer—Dutch farmers'—territories in South Africa to its own. To the surprise of the British army, which since the Crimean War (1853–1856) had not fought Europeans with weapons as modern as their own, the vastly outnumbered and outgunned Boers put up a fierce resistance for their homeland, defeating several columns of British regulars and besieging fortress towns. Britain's reputation in the family of nations was greatly hurt by what much of the world saw as imperial aggression. In the course of the war, which finally ended in 1902 with the capitulation of the Boers, the

British had invented the concentration camp for innocent Boer civilians, and the Boers had perfected guerilla warfare. Both are terrible legacies of the early twentieth century. The Irish were divided about the Boer War. Many supported the empire, but a significant minority, especially in Ireland, supported the Boers' right to be an independent republic.

In 1901, Queen Victoria (1819–1901), who had given her name to the age, died. At the time of her death, the British Empire—thanks to the Industrial Revolution, liberal capitalism, and superior technology—sprawled across the surface of the earth. Every inhabited continent had British colonies or dominions. In South Asia alone, what is now India, Pakistan, Bangladesh, Sri Lanka, and Myanmar owed allegiance to the British crown and were ruled by that island off the western coast of Europe: Great Britain. A few thousand British administrators, a small professional army augmented by native troops, and the Royal Navy maintained worldwide British hegemony. After the post–World War I treaty of Versailles in 1919, even more peoples were added to the empire.

But in Ireland, the beginning of the twentieth century brought a strong desire for home rule or, better still, complete independence from Britain. The Sinn Fein Party was established in 1908, and subsequently three illegal armies were formed in 1913: the pro-British Ulster Volunteer Force in the North and, in the South, the Irish Citizens Army and the Irish Volunteers. The island was racked with labor strikes as, disastrously, in 1914 the Parliament in Westminster put off home rule for Ireland until the cessation of World War I, when it was to be implemented after the peace treaty, with a Northern Ireland Parliament and another for the rest of the country. But it was too late for the Nationalists, for in the fateful year of 1916, men from the Irish Revolutionary Brotherhood and the Irish Citizen Army proclaimed the Irish Republic in Dublin on April 24 and fought the British army for five days. The subsequent drawn-out execution of 15 Republican prisoners from the Easter Rising shocked and galvanized the Irish majority into support of full independence from Britain even as thousands of Irishmen from Ulster and from the South were dying for Britain in the trenches of France and Belgium.

In December 1918, Republicans were victorious in general elections, and they convened an illegal Irish parliament, the Dail Eireann, in Dublin in January 1919. Simultaneously, the Anglo-Irish War, the Irish War of Independence, broke out with martial law instituted by the occupation forces. Meanwhile, ambushes, atrocities, and burnings marked a savage guerrilla war between Republicans and the Royal Irish Constabulary supported by the notorious Black and Tans, a paramilitary force of British ex-soldiers attempting on orders from London to terrorize the Irish into submission. But the Irish guerrillas were victorious, and the war-weary British finally requested a peace conference in 1921.

The Anglo-Irish Treaty providing for the partition of Ireland into the Free State in the South with Ulster remaining as a part of the United Kingdom was approved by the Dail in 1922. However, the tragic Irish Civil War ensued as Anti-Treaty Republicans fought the new government army and were defeated. The new state thus was tragically born in the blood of those who had fought together against the British and then killed each other. Hostilities finally ceased in 1923, while the efforts of the illegal underground Irish Republican Army (IRA) continue to this day to negate the terms of the treaty and force Britain out of Northern Ireland.

During the nine-year reign of King Edward VII (1841–1910) and the next four years after his death with King George V (1865–1936) on the throne, the United Kingdom, which then included Ireland, enjoyed a period of predominance, peace, prosperity, and progress that was looked back on as the "Edwardian Summer" preceding the conflagration of World War I. The only event that seemed in retrospect to have shaken British confidence and presaged the catastrophes to come was the foundering of the *Titanic* in 1912.

World War I (1914–1918) ended in victory for Great Britain and its allies—France, Italy, and the United States—but the nation was exhausted by the great loss of life and the enormous war debt. After the Anglo-Irish Treaty, the Kingdom of Great Britain and Northern Ireland entered on a between-the-wars period of social unrest: a general strike in 1926, disarmament, pacifism, economic depression, and a constitutional crisis that resulted in the abdication of King Edward VIII (1895–1972) in 1936, only a few months after his father's death.

Under a new constitution, the Irish Free State became Eire in 1937. As World War II broke out, Eire declared neutrality and skillfully managed to keep out of the war despite Anglo-American pressure and the German bombing of Dublin. But because of outdated economic and social policies, Ireland did not participate fully in the postwar European recovery.

With the outbreak of World War II in September 1939, Britain was yet again engaged in a life-and-death struggle with Germany. Under the indomitable Winston Churchill (1874–1965), Britain survived blitzkreig and blitz until the Soviet Union and the United States joined the fray in 1941. The Allied victory over Nazi Germany in 1945 left Europe devastated and Britain drained of wealth and will.

In 1949, the Irish Republic was declared with the hope and intention of bringing internal peace to the island, but in the 1950s and 1960s, the IRA continued its sporadic harassment of Britain and Northern Ireland, while the Ulster government allowed economic discrimination and occasional intimidation of its Catholic minority.

In 1952, the accession of the young Queen Elizabeth II (1926–) upon the death of her father King George VI (1895–1952) seemed to revitalize Britain, but the Suez crisis, in which Britain and France seized the canal in order to prevent its nationalization under the Egyptian government, ended in a humiliating withdrawal under pressure from the world community. That event signaled the end of Great Britain as a first-class world power, while the United States and the Soviet Union rivaled for world hegemony. But during the Cold War (1947–1991), Britain remained America's staunchest and most valuable ally.

The exhausted British, having given up India in 1947, no longer could either afford or control the other colonies, and a succession of partitions, withdrawals, and wars of liberation over 20 years drained the empire away. It was replaced by the British Commonwealth, a loose organization consisting of Britain, the dominions, and many former colonies. It is devoted to economic and cultural ties. Beginning in the 1960s large numbers of people from the former colonies emigrated to Great Britain, settling primarily in London and the industrial cities of the North and turning Britain, for the first time, into a multiethnic and multicultural society.

In 1955, Ireland joined the United Nations and in 1961 tried but failed to be admitted to the European Economic Community. Finally, Ireland was added to the European Union in 1973.

A significant social change came to Britain after the recommendations of the 1957 Wolfenden Report on homosexuality and prostitution sparked a decade of long-overdue legislation, eventually establishing, with the Sexual Offences Act of 1967, that any sexual behavior between consenting adults in private could not be considered criminal. The closet had opened for those who chose to come out. In 1968, after some 400 years, theater censorship was abolished in Great Britain. Set up to fight discrimination in 1967, the Northern Irish Civil Rights Association signaled a new militancy for the Catholic minority in Ulster, and the "Troubles" began the next year, lasting until the truce of 1994. The years between 1968 and now have seen assassinations of British officials and soldiers, IRA bombing campaigns in Britain, hunger strikes by IRA members in prison, loyalist opposition to possible Anglo-Irish agreements, and "Bloody Sunday," in which British soldiers shot to death 14 Nationalist marchers, and "Bloody Friday," in which an IRA bomb killed 11 in Belfast, both events occurring in 1972.

But the Republic of Ireland moves on. The "special position" of the Roman Catholic Church has been eliminated from the constitution. A referendum has permitted the introduction of divorce into Irish society for the first time since 1925. Membership in the European Union has helped Ireland economically, and the country is more prosperous than it has ever been in its history. It, like Britain, is also becoming a multiethnic, multicultural nation.

With an outstanding educational system, some of the most fertile land in Europe, close connections with America as well as the rest of Europe, burgeoning high-tech industries, and the youngest population in Europe, Ireland has entered the twenty-first century with high hopes and great expectations.

Britain also joined the European Union in 1973, bringing the nation closer to its continental neighbors than it had been since the loss of its last possessions in France during the sixteenth century. Devoid of most colonial possessions and responsibilities and identifying more with continental Europe, the United Kingdom significantly reduced its military and naval forces despite its commitment to NATO.

In 1982, however, when the Argentine military junta, believing Great Britain no longer had the will or the power to hold the Falkland Islands, seized the islands, the British lion roared once more. Britain mounted a powerful relief armada that sailed over 7,000 miles to the South Atlantic, where it inflicted a humiliating defeat on Argentina while freeing the islands and its English-speaking population.

A new patriotism came out of the Falkland experience, and the United Kingdom decided to rearm in order to project significant British power when necessary anywhere in the world. In the 1991 Gulf War to liberate Kuwait from Iraqi conquest and in the 2003 Gulf War to liberate Iraq from tyrannical rule, Great Britain stood by the United States as its chief ally, but Ireland remained neutral as usual. A new era of Anglo-American friendship and collaboration commenced as Americans and Britons recognized their commonality of values, culture, and world perspective. Meanwhile, the traditional friendship between Ireland and the United States continues to grow. Today, Britain and Ireland are friendly neighbors, sharing a language and much in the way of culture.

1

John Millington Synge
*The Playboy of the
Western World*
1907

In order to set a high standard and sustain itself over time, a great national theater has to have a great playwright at its inception or in its early years. The Comédie-Française had Molière in the seventeenth century, the Moscow Art Theater had Chekhov at the end of the nineteenth century, and the Irish National Theatre had John Millington Synge (1871–1909) at the beginning of the twentieth century. His greatest play was his first full-length poetic comedy, *The Playboy of the Western World*, in which Synge introduced the peasant play, the future staple of Irish theater. *The Playboy of the Western World* is the glory of early twentieth-century Irish drama and the most frequently performed and read Irish play of that period. *The Playboy of the Western World* is the finest Irish comedy just as Oscar Wilde's Victorian *The Importance of Being Earnest* is the finest English comedy. Of course, both plays were written by Irishmen, and both are ultimately about language. They depict the profound incongruity between the poetry and wit of a cleverly crafted story and the realities of life that words distort or incompletely signify.

The early international recognition of modern Irish drama as a major contributor to world theater and literature rested on the handful of plays Synge left behind. A generation later, Sean O'Casey renewed and enhanced that recognition.

BIOGRAPHICAL CONTEXT

In his drama, John Millington Synge (1871–1909), as much as any Irish dramatist of his time, captured the harsh truths, the painful lives, the soothing blind faith, the poetry of the oral tradition, and the humor of the poor folk of rural Ireland at the beginning of the twentieth century. Synge's plays, although often comic, are melancholy works. The heroes are sweet-talking men who try to win the women of their choice out of their staid domestic worlds into the adventure of life. His plays, so full of truth they hurt, were always controversial events in their initial receptions and often long after.

Edmund John Millington Synge was born of Protestant stock at Newton Little, Rathfarnham, County Dublin, to a lawyer and Galway landowner, John Hatch Synge, who died a year after Synge was born, and Katheen Traill Synge, a daughter of an evangelical Ulster Protestant clergyman. Synge, the youngest of five children, grew up and spent much of his life among women: mother, grandmother, sister, and servants—thus the strong older women in his plays. As a boy, he evidenced a great love for nature and frequently roamed the Dublin mountains and the forested glens of County Wicklow. After early private education, he attended Trinity College, Dublin, where he first studied natural science and where he also won prizes in Irish and Hebrew. Simultaneously, he studied at the Dublin's Royal Irish Academy of Music, becoming an Academy orchestra member and a violinist determined on a career as a professional musician. At this phase of his life, he rejected his inherited formal religion to become an individualistic lover of nature, a mystic, and an aesthete.

In pursuit of advanced musical training, Synge journeyed to Germany in 1893, where, after two years of study, he suddenly decided on a writer's career. Thus, he settled in Paris, then the center of European culture and literature. However, on vacation he visited Ireland's west coast and made his first trip out to the Aran Islands. Back in Paris in 1896, he met the great Irish poet William Butler Yeats, who advised him to return to Ireland, especially to the Aran Islands, to find his subjects in the narratives and language of his native land.

From 1899 to 1902, Synge was a regular and accepted summer visitor on the islands, listening, observing, and taking notes on the ancient and isolated life of the fisher folk. Synge's first book, *The Aran Islands* (1907), was illustrated by Yeats's talented brother and one of Ireland's greatest painters, Jack B. Yeats. Meanwhile, Synge began to write plays for the new Irish National Theatre. Synge's two one-act plays, *The Shadow of the Glen* (1903) and *Riders to the Sea* (1904), were brilliant first efforts in a genre completely new to him. Though they were received with anger and derision at home, the plays were greeted warmly in London by critics who saw in Synge's fresh and vigorous use of the Irish English language of farmers and fishermen a portent of great beginnings for the new Irish theater.

Although Synge first heard the story behind *The Shadow of the Glen* on Inishmaan in the Aran Islands, he chose to set his play in a Wicklow glen near his home, Glenmalure. The story of a jealous old man pretending to be dead in order to test the fidelity of his young wife, however, is an ancient one, as is the tale of the eternal triangle of an old husband, a young wife, and a young lover. Both have been used for tragedy and comedy, and both contribute to Synge's plot. Nora Burke's old husband, Dan, is distasteful to her. Their marriage was based on her desire to have some security in her life, while, in the pattern of Irish marriages of the past, Dan, "with a bit of a farm with cows on it, and sheep on the back hills," had waited until late in life to marry a young, strong, and desirable woman.

Tricked into believing that the husband, Dan, is dead, Nora and her young lover, Michael, plan to take his money and marry. Michael is concerned primarily with the money. Dan "rises from the dead" and orders Nora out of his house. The cowardly, parsimonious Michael won't go out into the world with the penniless woman. Instead, she departs with a passing tramp, who promises her sun, song, and a good companion in bed. Instead of falling to blows, the husband and the former lover are content in the end to drink to each other's health. The play is truly an Irish comedy, for at the close the vital woman seems superfluous as the old and young farmers are content in their friendship and their whiskey.

The only play of Synge's set in the Aran Islands, *Riders to the Sea* is the playwright's darkest, most tragic drama. The presence of irrevocable fate is so strong in the play that, for the first and only time in a Synge drama, language and character are placed second to plot. Central to the drama is the character of Maurya, one of the first generic, all-suffering, all-sacrificing Irish mothers in modern Irish drama. She has given her husband and a son to the sea, and now she must watch helplessly as yet another son, Bartley, her last, rides his horses down to the shore and into the eternity that the sea symbolizes. Maurya tells her story as she provides coffins for the dead and begins her mournful keening. Men, cut off in their prime, continually enter the cemetery of the sea as Maurya reminds us, "There does be a power of young men floating round in the sea." The tragic conclusion of *Riders to the Sea* is the most ancient and the greatest grief: the death of the child before the parent.

After the opening of the Abbey Theatre in 1904, Synge became one of its directors, and the next year *The Well of the Saints* was first produced in the new theater. For this play, Synge's knowledge of French literature served him well, as *The Well of the Saints* is based in part on a French Morality Play of the fifteenth century. His two blind, indigent protagonists, Martin and

Mary Doul, surely inspired Beckett's creation of the beggarly pair, Estragon and Vladimir, in Samuel Beckett's *Waiting for Godot*. The blind couple are a happy couple despite their affliction. They rant, rave, and abuse each other, but they live contentedly in their own world, and it is a rich, variegated, and beautiful one because it exists in their colorful imaginations. They each believe, for example, that the other is very attractive whereas in fact they are far from it.

Then a saint at a holy well miraculously restores their sight, and although at first they are delighted, they soon come to realize each other's and then their own ugliness. They also see how unpleasant looking and acting the sighted are. They no longer have a great deal to say to each other. Their lives are now individually different. Now they must work for a living. Mary and Martin separate for a while, but as their sight dims again, they rediscover each other and reunite in their happy relationship. Therefore, they spurn the interfering saint, his asceticism, and his miracles. Mary's curtain line sums it all up: "The Lord protect us from the Saints of God."

In 1907, *The Playboy of the Western World*, Synge's masterpiece, provoked a riot at its Abbey opening as nationalists objected to its portrayal of the Irish character, and others objected to the mention of a woman's undergarment in public. Synge's last completed play, *The Tinker's Wedding*, was written in 1902 and published in 1908, but it was not produced by the Abbey in Synge's lifetime because of its anticlerical scenes.

The Rabelaisian comedy pits Michael Byrne, a crafty tinker—that is, an Irish traveler, a person of the roads who lives like a gypsy—against a priest who wants to extract as much money and goods for his services as he can. The tinker's companion, Sarah Casey, craves middle-class respectability and thus wishes to be married. Michael reluctantly agrees to marry because, like a bourgeois, he has economic reasons for tying up his woman as wife. She is good at selling, and unless married, she might leave him for another man.

The priest is willing to marry the couple for the seemingly bargain price of half a sovereign, but he also wants a can (drinking vessel) that the tinker (a traditional pot mender and tinsmith) is making. Michael tries to trick the priest out of the can, but the priest then refuses to marry the couple and orders them off. The tinkers tie him, gag him with the bag that had held the can, and run for their lives. Michael and Sarah will continue to live as before, although they pledge their troth to each other in a "Tinker's Wedding." The delightfully farcical play feels and sounds like a medieval folk play.

Synge was engaged to the actress Maire O'Neill when he died of Hodgkin's disease on March 24, 1909, before completing his last play, *Deidre of the Sorrows*, a play based on Irish mythology with a deadly triangle of an old man, his young bride, and her young lover. Conchubor, the cuckolded king, is like a darker King Arthur, and his jealousy-inspired treachery in luring the heroine and the hero back to Ireland from Scotland results in the suicide of Deidre and her lover. Lady Gregory and Yeats completed Synge's tragedy.

Synge's plays were a success in London even before his death, and the Abbey company took *The Playboy of the Western World* to America, where it provoked more riots—this time by irate Irish Americans—and achieved everlasting fame.

PLOT DEVELOPMENT

The setting of *The Playboy of the Western World* is a country public house (bar) in Mayo whose publican (owner) is Michael Flaherty. But it is his daughter Pegeen who runs the establishment and who does most of the work. She is betrothed to Shawn Keogh, an unattractive, cowardly, priest-ridden cousin for whom neither she nor the audience have much respect. Pegeen is preparing for her wedding, and the couple are only waiting for a disposition from the church because they are cousins. Michael is more enthusiastic about the match than Pegeen is because Shawn is a relatively affluent farmer.

Michael Flaherty is about to leave for a wake with friends, but timorous Shawn does not think it proper that he be left alone in the house with Pegeen. A pitiful fugitive, Christy Mahon, comes into the house asking if the police come there often. Michael assures him that they don't. Everyone in the pub quizzes him as to why he is on the run from the law, and reluctantly he announces that he has murdered his father, a farmer like himself.

The unprepossessing young man becomes an instant hero to Pegeen and the community. Even an older woman, the wily Widow Quin, sets her cap for him. But Christy soon cares for Pegeen, and she falls in love with the young "hero," who conjectures, "Wasn't I the foolish fellow not to kill my father in the years gone by?" He delights in telling the story of the murder, to any and all, embellishing it with each accounting. Pegeen drives off all the other women who would like to get close to the handsome and seemingly brave lad.

Shawn tries but fails to bribe his rival into leaving the area with a passage to America and new clothes. Widow Quin is willing to help Shawn—for a price—by marrying Christy, but he will have no one but Pegeen. When Michael returns, Christy convinces him that he, not Shawn, should be allowed to marry Pegeen. Michael is leery at first. After all, Christy is a parricide. But finally he agrees.

After preening himself and milking the situation, the now cocky Christy finds his story finally unraveling when his father appears, head slightly dented but very much alive. Old Mahon proceeds to beat his son. Christy, who actually believed he had killed his father, now has lost face with Pegeen and the community, and so to recover his standing, he takes his father outside and "kills" him again. But this time the community is aghast, for, as Pegeen says, "There's a great gap between a gallous story and a dirty deed." A "romantic" story about murdering one's father in some far-off place is one thing. But the reality, with all its immorality, sinfulness, horror, and the community's possible culpability for sheltering the criminal, is another thing indeed. The men of the village try to put a rope around Christy's neck, and Pegeen even burns him to break his hold on a table. She no longer wants Christy.

A noose is finally placed over Christy's head, and he is about to be dragged off to the police. But tough Old Mahon is still not "killed." He reappears and is full of admiration for his son now because in confronting his father, Christy has proved his manhood to him.

Christy now disdains Pegeen and the community, and he marches off with his father following respectfully. The young hero has, in the tradition of comedy, overcome the impediment of paternal power. But poor Pegeen, full of regret for having turned on her lover, laments the lament of many a young Irish woman at that time: "Oh, my grief, I've lost him surely. I've lost the only playboy of the Western World." The "Western World," of course, is the west of Ireland.

CHARACTER DEVELOPMENT

Christy Mahon's character and development are finely drawn. His dramatic action is a masterly example of the triumph of youth over such impediments as a brutal father. The overcoming is an essential characteristic of all romantic comedy from Menander's New Comedy in ancient Greece through Shakespeare's romantic comedies like *Twelfth Night* and *As You Like It* and right down to the present day.

Christy evolves from what Old Mahon describes as a "dribbling idiot" to become not only a manly youth but also a sports hero and a poet-hero like the ancient bards of Ireland. He has two fine women fighting over him because they believe he has had the courage to kill his hard-hearted father, something many Irish men and not a few women would have liked to do but, of course, didn't. For the first time in his life, Christy sees himself reflected in the eyes of young women as handsome and desirable. His only regret is that he hadn't killed his father years ago.

Yet a part of Christy's charm is that he has some feminine characteristics, and so a factor in his attraction to the women of County Mayo is that he is not a drinking, blustering, macho bully. He is slight in build and speaks with a small voice. Christy likes to look in a mirror and is very proud of the new clothes he has tricked out of Shawn. Pegeen says he is "a soft lad," and softness is easy to like in a rough land and a population that has little of it.

Margaret (Pegeen Mike) Flaherty has the devil's own tongue and temper. She is bitter because her father intends for her to marry a man who has wealth but whom she does not love. She is also angry because she has to run the pub as well as do all the household chores, which her mother would have done if she were still alive. Pegeen has a touch of the masculine in her. She drives off the other women and girls who are after Christy. She does not hide her disdain for Shawn or her disappointment with her heavy-drinking and less-than-responsible father. When it appears that her beau, Christy, did not kill his father, she no longer wants to marry him. And when he seems to have finally done "Da" in, she is the only one of the crowd "man" enough to burn him with a smoldering piece of sod to get him to release his grip on a table so that he could be hauled away to be hanged. Her pride, vanity, and perhaps her lack of femininity cause her to lose the best man she could have had for a husband and face the awful possibility of a life with the unattractive Shawn.

Michael Flaherty at first finds Christy a threat to the dowry that Shawn will give him for Pegeen. In addition, a man who has killed his father is naturally not the sort of person he wants for a son-in-law. But eventually he accepts the possible match between his daughter and Christy because he is sure the lovers will produce grandchildren he would be proud of. Pegeen has little affection for him, however, because of the selfish way he has used her and because of his drinking.

Widow Quin, like Pegeen is a strong, combative, and self-sufficient woman. She desires another husband, even though she caused the death of her first one. But she really cares for Christy, and when she realizes he won't marry her because he loves young Pegeen, she tries to save him from his father's revenge by first diverting the raging old man and then trying to hide Christy in woman's clothing so that he might escape the police. In many ways, Widow Quin is the most likable character in the play.

Shawn Keogh is a craven, timorous man, truly unworthy of marriage to a feisty young colleen like Pegeen Mike. From the early moments of the play, the audience hopes that Pegeen won't have to marry him. In the end, when Shawn gloats to Pegeen that the local priest will be able to marry them now, he receives a box on the ear for his troubles. Still it seems that he has won after all, for what other choice does the heartbroken girl have?

Old Mahon is a stereotypical, patriarchal Irish father. His type is found again and again in a dramatic tradition that is hard on fathers, especially those who are small-property owners and who struggle on a hard land. He has driven all his children away except Christy, the one too weak-willed to leave him until the thought of being married off to an old widow woman drove him to attempt murder. When Old Manon is finally defeated by his youngest son—after two bashes on the head, either of which might have killed a weaker man—the audience rejoices in the justice of the minirevolution against brutal, unjust, and self-serving authority. And as this is a comedy, Old Mahon rejoices too.

It must be said that those Irish people and Irish Americans who early in the twentieth century objected to the portrait of the rural Irish character in *The Playboy of the Western World* were aware that Synge came from the Protestant landowner class and a suburban Dublin environment. They felt his portrayal of the rural Irish as having false values and being easily fooled a supercilious and biased one. The dreary final scene of a drab community of half-drunk peasant men and frustrated women was a bit hard to swallow despite the laughs.

THEMES

A major theme of *The Playboy of the Western World* is the stagnation of provincial life caused by inertia resulting from the crushing alliance of the Church and the British government, the remoteness of the West, the lack of education, and the loss of the "brightest and the best" of young people through emigration. Young Irish women who remained behind on the insufficient and worn-out land were especially hurt by the fact that far more young men than women emigrated, and those who remained behind could afford only to marry late or not at all.

Then there are the marriage wars between families, or between competing men over women with dowries, or between women over the few eligible and desirable men. After all, for Margaret (Pegeen) Flaherty, Christy was "the only Playboy of the Western World." Related to the theme of marriage wars is the struggle of the young to overcome the impediment of parentally arranged marriages to maintain or acquire farm property, when the young often desired to pursue their own destinies. Pegeen's father has been pushing her into marrying the prosperous but wimpy Shawn Keoh, and sadly, it seems, she may have to marry Shawn after all, for the life of an unmarried peasant woman in rural island at the end of the nineteenth century was not an enviable one.

Another theme in *The Playboy of the Western World* is that of the violence in Irish society at the time of the play. Synge treats the tendency toward violence satirically in *The Playboy of the Western World*—Christy is unable to murder his father in two tries. The peasants who first exalted Christy as a "killer" later tried to have him hanged. But rural Ireland was angry indeed over the rule of Anglo-Irish landlords.

A lighter perennial theme in *The Playboy of the Western World* and throughout modern Irish drama is the love of the Irish for taking flights of fancy and letting imagination have its head. Storytelling with gusto and embellishment is a relished art form.

NARRATIVE STYLE

The form of *The Playboy of the Western World* is a succession of brilliant conversations and narration interspersed with episodes of action that lead up to the double reversal of the climax: Christy evoking the hatred of his former admirers and brought down for "killing" his father a second time and, when "Da" is "resurrected," rising to manhood and leading his father off in triumph, thus leaving a forlorn Pegeen lamenting his departure.

The Playboy of the Western World is a superb blend of tragicomedy and thwarted romance. It is full of irony. Imagine a people so starved for excitement or variety that they would puff up a starving wretch of a boy and make him a hero first for parricide and a scapegoat next to cover the community's shortcomings. In *The Playboy of the Western World*, Synge succeeded in his stated goal: to write in an English that seems to be perfectly Irish in essence, almost as if it were translated from the Gaelic. Synge created a form of Irish English that is prose-poetry. Characters employ startling and evocative figures of speech that are quite far from realistic conversation. The heightened language, the poetic imagery, the broad characterizations, the humor, the precise structure, the inversion of values, and the satire of the play are so excellent that without doubt the play is not only a masterpiece but also the greatest single play ever to have been written in Ireland.

HISTORICAL CONTEXT

In the late 1800s, the time of the play, massive and cruel evictions of poor Irish tenant farmers by Anglo-Irish landlords were taking place. The evictions, sometimes violent, led to rent strikes, boycotts of British and Anglo-Irish products, and outbreaks of retaliatory guerrilla warfare. The Royal Irish Constabulary, supporting the British government, was constantly on the march in the western counties such as Mayo, the setting for the play. In addition, unemployed and homeless men were wandering the land looking for work and, when not finding it, resorting to theft. Thus, at the opening of the play, Pegeen has every right to be afraid to be left in the family pub while her father and his friends go off to get drunk at a wake.

Irish violence in the late nineteenth and early twentieth centuries also took shape in Fenian activities. The Fenians, also known as the Irish Republican Brotherhood (IRB), an underground organization dedicated to overthrowing British rule violently and establishing the Irish Republic, used assassination as one of its methods of intimidating the Anglo-Irish power structure. Their methods were to a large extent unsuccessful, but the repressive measures of the British government to stem IRB activities caused fear and anger in the general population of Ireland. Clashes between police and militia on one side and a frustrated population on the other kept violence on a slow boil, but clashes were frequent and inevitable.

SUGGESTED READINGS

Greene, David H., and Edward M. Stephens. *J. M. Synge 1871–1909*. New York: Macmillan, 1959.

King, Mary C. *The Drama of J. M. Synge*. Syracuse, N.Y.: Syracuse University Press, 1985.

Synge, John Millington. *The Playboy of the Western World*. New York: Communications Group, 1997.

2

George Bernard Shaw
Saint Joan
1923

Always the intellectual playwright, George Bernard Shaw (1856–1950) wrote *Saint Joan* because he felt that previous commentators on Joan's life misunderstood the importance of her actions. Shaw believed that Joan was a rebel against the Roman Catholic Church, a proto-Protestant so to speak, who claimed and exercised the right to communicate directly with Heaven. In addition, Joan's actions in support of a French nationalist state against foreign invaders, the English, foreshadowed the rise of nationalism elsewhere in Europe. It is no coincidence that Shaw, an Irishman, was writing *Saint Joan* while the Irish people were liberating themselves from 700 years of British rule and facing a brutal civil war.

From its first performance, *Saint Joan* was recognized as a masterpiece. More than any other of Shaw's plays, it made Shaw the obvious choice for the Nobel Prize for Literature in 1925. Throughout the decades since its debut, *Saint Joan* has received respect and admiration almost akin to Shakespeare's great tragedies because, as in the tradition of great tragic heroes like Hamlet and Lear, Joan's suffering is not merely imposed and passively accepted. She incurs it by her own decision. Critics and audiences have found that although evil is temporarily triumphant in *Saint Joan*, the young woman conquers because her spirit remains unbroken.

BIOGRAPHICAL CONTEXT

Like his fellow Dublin-born playwright Oscar Wilde (1854–1900), George Bernard Shaw had a distinctly Irish wit but made his contribution to the drama and the theater in England. Most significantly, Shaw brought intel-lectual drama to the English stage. Shaw was born into the Protestant lower middle class, the one son and third child of a heavy-drinking, continually fail-ing merchant named George Carr Shaw, and Elizabeth Gurly Shaw, a woman who had pretensions to a career as a singer. Her music teacher, George Vandeleur Lee, moved into the family home on Upper Synge Street (33 Synge Street) and formed the other leg of a marital triangle.

Shaw's education was mediocre. After early tutoring, at 10 he began to attend the Wesleyan Connexional School in Dublin. At 12, he was placed in a school in Dalkey, the village south of Dublin where Lee owned a cottage and where the "extended" family spent summers. Because money was scarce in the household, Shaw was transferred to the Central Model School in Dublin, where to his horror he had to associate with working-class Catholic children. The fact that those children were Catholics did not bother Shaw as much as their working-class status. It was a clear sign of his family's fall. His last school was the Dublin English Scientific and Commercial Day School, in which he prepared for clerking. Unfortunately, Shaw, always a middling student, could not even think of seeking admission to prestigious Trinity College, Dublin, where bright Protestant young men were prepared for leader-ship in the cultural and political spheres, because he could not have passed the entrance examinations, nor could his father have paid the tuition. Thus, Shaw had to go to work at age 15.

With formal schooling over, Shaw began his self-education with reading, going as often as he could to view the art in the nearby National Gallery of Ireland, and enjoying the music his mother, sisters—who were also musicians—and Lee brought into the otherwise unhappy home. Shaw became very knowledgeable about music and even taught himself to play the violin.

His first job, which he hated, was as a junior clerk in a land office. At 16, he was a clerk in a business office. When her music teacher departed for London, Mrs. Shaw and the girls quickly followed. Shaw was left with his father for four years. Unhappy and disgusted with his father's drinking, in 1876 he joined his mother and her lover in London, where she supported him while he wrote one unsuccessful novel after another. Shaw did not return to Ireland for nearly 30 years. For nine years of literary effort, he earned almost nothing.

Moved by the plight of London's poor, Shaw joined the Fabian Society—a group of intellectual, moderate socialists who advocated evolutionary change rather than Marxist revolutionary class conflict—and became an effective speaker for socialism. William Archer, the drama critic and theorist, found Shaw work as a book reviewer. Shaw also became a successful music critic.

Shaw turned to playwriting in 1892 with *Widowers' Houses,* his provocative attack on slumlords, followed by *Arms and the Man* (1894), an antiwar comedy, and *Candida* (1897), a humorous debate between poetry and conventionality. His first commercial success was *The Devil's Disciple* (1897), a satire on courtship as well as nineteenth-century romantic drama. Other provocative plays include *Mrs. Warren's Profession* (1902), a scathing indictment of those who profit from prostitution, followed by *Man and Superman* (1903), in which Shaw extols the superiority of women; *Major Barbara* (1905), a play about the moral dilemma in accepting "tainted" money with which one can do good; *Caesar and Cleopatra* (1906), Shaw's comic prequel to Shakespeare's *Antony and Cleopatra;* and the perennially popular *Pygmalion* (1914).

The musical comedy version of *Pygmalion,* Alan J. Lerner and Frederick Loewe's *My Fair Lady,* has made the plot of this play his best known. *Pygmalion* is based on the legend about an ancient Greek sculptor of that name who falls in love with an ivory statue he has made of a beautiful girl. He prays to the gods to give it life, and when they do, he calls the living girl Galatea, and he marries her.

In the play, Professor Henry Higgins, an affluent, eccentric expert in phonetics, overhears a flower girl speaking with an atrocious cockney accent. As he "collects" her by taking phonetic notes, passersby think he is a policeman and try to defend her. One of them is Colonel Pickering, a retired officer in the British Indian army who is an authority on Indian languages and who has, coincidentally, come to London to seek out the famous professor. The men are delighted to meet each other, so Higgins gives the girl, whose name is Liza Doolittle, some money to stop her whining.

Feeling flush, she takes a cab home. However, she has overheard the professor boast that he could teach her to speak so well that he could pass her off as a duchess in three months. The next day, she arrives at his house and tries to hire him—with the money he gave her—to teach her to sound upper class. Pickering bets Higgins that he can't do it well enough to indeed pass her off as an aristocrat. Liza, somewhat fearfully, for Higgins is a bully, agrees to the scheme.

Higgins and Pickering train Liza for a period and then send her off on a test run to Higgins's mother's house where she also meets a Mrs. Eynsford Hill, her daughter, and her son Freddie, who immediately is taken by the now well-scrubbed and tastefully dressed girl. At this point, Liza has only two subjects to talk about: the weather and the bad health of relatives.

Higgins next takes Liza to a ball and wins his bet. The men are deliriously happy and ignore Liza, who grows furious. She, a "New Woman," flings his slippers at the demanding Higgins and flees to his mother's house. Higgins

follows, seeking Liza's return, but it is clear that she will no longer be patron-
ized by him. Instead, she'll either marry Freddy or teach other cockney flower
girls to speak like duchesses. Liza thus triumphs over the selfish, patriarchal
professor.

It is clear that there is no romance between Liza and Higgins in Shaw's
play. Shaw states in a postscript that Liza marries Freddie and they go into
business together. However, the films and the American musical theater
could not accept Shaw's unromantic position and invariably changed his
ending.

In 1898, Shaw married the Anglo-Irish heiress Charlotte Payne-
Townshend. In World War I, Shaw was an ardent and outspoken pacifist.
As a result, he was blackballed by society and nearly imprisoned. Fame and
popularity returned after the war with such plays as *Heartbreak House* (1919),
in which Shaw predicts the doom of the British upper class, and his greatest
dramatic achievement, *Saint Joan* (1923). Shaw received the Nobel Prize
for Literature in 1925. The Shaws had no children. Charlotte Shaw died in
1943. He continued writing up to his death in 1945.

Shaw was an Ibsenite. He took Henrik Ibsen's (1828–1906) concept of
the thesis play, in which a problem of society is presented for consideration
by the society itself—represented by the middle-class audience. He employed
the concept in social comedies that sparkled with wit, clever situations, and
wonderful dialogue. Most significantly, Shaw's "Quintessence of Ibsenism"
(1891) not only delineated the Norwegian's iconoclastic purposes in attacking
hypocritical bourgeois society's values but also crystallized Shaw's political
and artistic agenda.

Shaw was a man of principle. He very much wanted to reform the world
according to his precepts and values. He had little use for those aesthetes, like
his early rival Oscar Wilde, who advocated art for art's sake. Early on, Shaw
presented the "New Woman"—educated, freethinking, and often professionally employed—as heroines in his plays. He vigorously supported women's
suffrage. Shaw made war on poverty. The great Shavian socialist paradox is
that poverty is deemed the worst of all crimes in a capitalist society.

Although Shaw's plays are discussion plays with ideas taking precedence
over action, his presentation is always dramatic. Polemics abound, but characters are true to life if eccentric. Shaw's dramaturgy is old-fashioned and
very modern too. His plays often followed the well-made play formula:
alternations of suspense and surprise, unexpected entrances, and astonish-
ing reversals. On the other hand, he was the first British dramatist to put an
automobile and an airplane (crashed) on the stage and to depict the effect of
an air raid on an English household.

Without doubt Shaw was the greatest playwright in the English language since Shakespeare.

PLOT DEVELOPMENT

Scene 1 is set in a room in the castle of Vaucouleurs on the River Meuse, between Lorraine and Champagne, on an early spring morning in 1429. Captain Robert de Baudricourt, a military squire, is angry with his steward because the latter has not located eggs for the captain's breakfast. The steward says that the girl from Lorraine is responsible. She has been at the door for two days waiting for an interview with Robert and has cast a spell on the castle so that the hens will not lay. He calls her in, and she states that the Lord has sent her to him in order that she receive a horse, armor, and soldiers to go with her to the court of Charles, the Dauphin (heir apparent) of France. Charles's father is dead, so he should now be king, but he is uncrowned. She believes that the Dauphin will give her troops with which to relieve the English siege of Orleans. Then she will accompany Charles to his coronation in Rheims Cathedral.

Robert sends Joan out and discusses the situation with Betrand de Poulengey, whom Joan nicknames Polly. The French need a miracle to save Orleans, and Polly thinks Joan can bring it off. Joan is recalled, and she states that the English soldiers are only men and that God wants them to return to their own country. She will unite the French and bring victory. The squire sends Joan on to Charles, and suddenly the castle hens commence laying again! A minor miracle?

Scene 2 is set in Chinon Castle, in Touraine, where the Dauphin is holding court. It is March 8, 1429. The Archbishop of Rheims and the Lord Chamberlain, Monseigneur de la Trémouille, vexed at waiting for the Dauphin, discuss his debts when Gilles de Rais, a happy young man who is known as Bluebeard, enters with news of the positive effect Joan has had on the troops. The Dauphin, Charles, enters with a letter from Robert stating that he has sent Charles a gift. It is Joan.

The Archbishop and the Chamberlain do not want Charles to receive Joan. Charles, at the suggestion of Bluebeard, has the courtier impersonate him. If Joan can spot the true royal in the crowd, then she must indeed have been sent by God. Joan enters in armor, sees through the disguise, and pulls Charles out of the crowd, stating that she has come to smash the English and make him king.

Alone with Joan, Charles confesses his inadequacies and asks her to depart and not to make him take command. But Joan insists she will give him courage.

He believes her, and calling back the court, Charles announces that he is giving Joan command of the French forces. Angered, Trémouille insists that he is in command. Charles now has courage. He snaps his fingers in the face of the Chamberlain, and Joan, with her sword held as a cross, falls on her knees and thanks God. Others follow her action.

Scene 3 is set on the south bank of the River Loire near Orleans. The date is April 29, 1429. Dunois, a French commander, is hoping that a west wind will spring up and replace the east wind so that he can move his troops by water. Joan, in armor, approaches, and the wind drops. She asks where the English are, and he replies that they are on all sides. Joan states that the French forces should sally out, cross the bridge, and attack at once. Her wish seems militarily impossible. Joan wants to go up the ladder to the English forts, holding up her sacred sword. Dunois says the forts must be attacked by water. The boats are ready, but the wind is wrong. Joan wants to be taken to a church to pray, but immediately the wind shifts. Another small miracle has taken place. Dunois believes God has spoken, and he will follow Joan's orders as the cheering men charge an English fort, calling out, "God and the Maid."

Scene 4 takes place in a tent in the English camp. The English commander, the Earl of Warwick, a 46-year-old soldier, is trying to enjoy a book, but his chaplain is fuming over the English defeats, including the loss of Orleans. Peter Cauchon, the Bishop of Beauvais, enters, and Warwick asks him if Joan is a sorceress, as his chaplain insists she must be in order to explain her survival in battle and her victories. Cauchon thinks that Joan is an instrument of the devil. She is not a witch but a heretic, and Cauchon would like to save her soul. Whether the French or the English win does not concern the Bishop, but Warwick realizes that Joan must be destroyed, or the English cause is doomed.

In a 15-minute verbal exchange among Warwick, the Bishop of Beauvais, and the jingoistic English monk de Stogumber, Shaw delineates all the conflicts of the play: Church against state, feudalism against nationalism, and Catholicism against an incipient Protestantism.

Scene 5's locale is at the coronation of Charles VII in the Cathedral of Rheims. Joan and the French clearly have won significant victories, although the English remain in the north. Joan, still in male attire, is kneeling in prayer. Dunois wants her to meet the people, but Joan wants Charles to have the glory of the moment. Dunois informs Joan that she is a source of jealousy in the court. But she has no interest in court politics and intends to go home to her farm after Paris is liberated. However, for now she still has confidence in her saintly voices.

Prissy Charles enters, complaining about his robes and the smell of the holy oil used to anoint him. He does not want Joan to go on to Paris. Rather, he would have peace with the Burgundians. The Archbishop of Rheims accuses Joan of the sin of pride. But Joan insists that God will still give her victories. Dunois is skeptical. He informs her that if she is taken captive, no one will rescue her. Joan insists that Charles would, but he informs her that he could not afford the ransom. The Archbishop warns her not to expect mercy from Couchan. Joan insists that she has always been alone. But the common people love her, and that will sustain her even if she goes to the stake. Poor Charles only wants her to shut up and go home.

Scene 6 takes place in a castle in Rouen on May 30, 1431. Joan has been captured nine months before by the Burgundians, and Warwick has bought her from them and turned her over to the ecclesiastical authorities. A room has been set up as a court. Bishop Cauchon and the Inquisitor are the judges, and there is no jury. Warwick is anxious to get the trial over. He will act on his own if necessary, but Cauchon and the Inquisitor are determined that Joan will have a "fair" trial. They want to save her soul. Only Ladvenu, a young monk, argues, but to no avail, that Joan is a simple girl and that saints have said as much as she has.

Joan is brought in wearing a page's uniform. Joan's heresy is particularly dangerous because her independent thinking could lead to Protestantism. Joan sees the executioner standing behind her, and she falls into despair. She now thinks that her voices have led her into this state and that they must be devils because God would not have her excommunicated and burned at the stake. The ecclesiastics are delighted. The English are furious at the thought that Joan may not be executed. Joan signs a confession to all charges brought against her, but then learns that she must spend the rest of her life in solitary confinement, where she will be deprived of light, nature, and the sound of church bells bringing her voices on the wind. She tears up the confession and is delivered over to the English for execution. Church law and state politics have crushed innocence.

Joan is put to the stake off stage. It is reported that an English soldier gave her a cross of sticks to hold on to and surely must be damned for doing that. Warwick wonders if he has heard the last of her.

The epilogue takes place during a June night in 1456, 25 years after Joan was executed. The setting is a chateau bedroom of 56-year-old Charles VII, now called Charles the Victorious. Charles is in bed with a book. He learns from Ladvenu, the kind monk, that Joan has been rehabilitated by a court. She appears in dim light and tells Charles that he is asleep and dreaming. Charles claims that she owes him thanks for getting justice for her at last, but now Cauchon appears and insists that he has been dishonored by the reversal. Now Joan learns from Dunois that the English have been driven from France.

A rowdy English soldier enters and announces that he gets one day off from hell annually because he did one good deed. Joan interrupts to say he gave a poor girl a cross of sticks as she stood at the stake. Warwick appears to congratulate Joan on her rehabilitation, saying that there was nothing personal in his actions. He made a political mistake, and because of it, Charles has his crown and Joan her halo.

Now a cleric from 1920 enters and reads out the canonization proclamation signed in the Vatican on May 16, 1920. All kneel to Joan, and she asks them if they would like her to return to earth. They all back off. Clearly, Joan is easier to take dead than alive. Joan is left with the soldier of the cross of sticks. Then he too leaves, and Joan stands alone, wondering how long it will be before the world is ready to receive its saints.

CHARACTER DEVELOPMENT

Shaw's Joan is one of the great characters of modern drama. She is his most perfect construction. Like Hamlet, Joan lives on in the Western imagination. She is Shaw's superwoman. His Joan has a nonconformist mind that thinks outside the medieval box. Ultimately, Shaw confirms that Joan of Arc is a light still shining.

Shaw portrays Joan as a farmer's daughter from Lorraine, uneducated but neither a fool, nor a madwoman hearing voices, nor a saint. She is intelligent, full of common sense, and high minded. Joan, like so many good and innocent young people in all eras, believes that she can change the world with her honesty, idealism, and enthusiasm. But the great medieval world of realpolitik—the powerful international Church, ambitious nobles, an implacably rigid society, and the laws and customs of men—was beyond her experience and comprehension.

When, out of her love for life, Joan temporarily denies her voices and allows that interpretation of God's will is the sole province of religious authority, she becomes a tragic figure trapped by fate. Realizing that the authorities plan life imprisonment for her in a dark cell, she chooses immediate death to a living one. At that moment, she entered not only history but also the imagination of Western culture. She will come to stand for independent thought and love of one's country. Immolation meant martyrdom and immortality, but they were of small importance to a poor girl who hardly understood why she was being killed.

There are no true villains in *Saint Joan*. All characters think they are acting in the best interests of society.

Charles, the Dauphin, later Charles VII of France, is a poor physical specimen, but he is intelligent and has a sense of humor. Nevertheless, he is craven and disloyal. At times, he seems like a spoiled child. It is only in the partly amusing epilogue that we come to realize how successful a politician he was. Joan taught him to be a man, but although he used Joan to win victories over the English, more importantly to Charles, Joan allowed him to conquer his own court.

The Earl of Warwick is a cultured, courteous, and proud English nobleman who serves the English cause as best he can and in any way he can. He also symbolizes secular privilege and entrenched feudalism. Warwick uses reason when he can, but he is not averse to using force if necessary.

Bishop Cauchon is a compassionate theologian, but he is totally committed to maintaining the supremacy of the Roman Catholic Church. He would not have Joan executed for political expediency, as would Warwick, and he would save Joan's soul if he could without compromising his rigid orthodoxy. But Joan's individualism is a threat to his church, and that is why she must die.

De Stogumber is crass. He is the personification of the English imperialist of the late nineteenth century. The English see themselves as naturally superior to all others. When made fun of for his narrow patriotism and limited vision, he never gets the joke. Only Joan's martyrdom unexpectedly changes De Stogumber and shakes his "faith" in his own sureties.

THEMES

Shaw the iconoclast presents as his most important theme in *Saint Joan* his belief that conservative society will always reject the moral genius that arises from time to time to rejuvenate a flaccid, weary, and cynical epoch. Joans are martyred because society will let charismatic moral leaders move it only so far. Then it destroys the leader before it is exhausted by goodness. Shaw says that the power brokers of society will not change even for saints.

Another important theme of the play is the debate between private conscience and public duty. No one, not even Warwick, hates Joan. Privately, many of those who condemned her did so with the greatest reticence, but they let their devotion to duty win out, wrongly of course, over their individual consciences. Joan's saintliness stems from the fact that she remains true to conscience, where the pure knowledge of right and wrong resides in all of us.

NARRATIVE STYLE

Saint Joan is the finest example of Shaw's unique variation on the formulaic nineteenth-century well-made play in which exposition is followed by complication and then resolution. Shaw added argument as the fourth unit in the formula. In *Saint Joan*, the epilogue is devoted to the argument that unconventional genius should be but, alas, is not understood, appreciated, and encouraged.

From early on in his career as a playwright, Shaw was aware that the printed versions of his plays would reach a larger audience than performances would. For an eagerly awaited edition of a play, Shaw wrote informative, clarifying, and highly political prefaces. Thus, *Saint Joan* in print received a 55-page preface in which Shaw indicates Joan's social position in her society and her place in the history of women; he discusses the question of her innocence or guilt; he argues that, despite her claiming to hear the voices of saints, she was a rationalist; and he insists that Joan dressed as a soldier not because she knew it would be easier to campaign in that garb instead of a woman's gown but because she wanted to lead a man's life.

Within the play text, Shaw's prose style and dialogue formation are masterly. That dialogue, an achievement of a lifetime of dramatic writing, though often longer than natural, is brilliantly lucid. In *Saint Joan*, despite the sensational subject matter and the fact that many passages in the play feel like pure poetry, Shaw always writes for the viewer's or reader's mind, not their hearts.

Shaw's characters speak with decorum; that is, they use diction and vocabulary appropriate to their class, occupation, and gender. Still there is always a pervading sense of formalism and the rhetorical mode in Shaw's heightened dramatic language. These factors help make *Saint Joan* the masterpiece that it is.

HISTORICAL CONTEXT

The full title of Shaw's play, *Saint Joan: A Chronicle Play in Six Scenes and an Epilogue*, indicates that the playwright thought of his drama in Shakespearean terms, for the history plays of Shakespeare's time were often called chronicles. Frequently, they dealt with events in the Middle Ages and the wars between England and France, as does *Saint Joan*.

Joan of Arc, or, for the French, Jeanne d'Arc, was a French peasant girl born about 1412 when the Hundred Years' War (1337–1453) raged on as England and France fought over the possession of the French crown. After several great English victories, the English were finally defeated. But in 1429, the English and their allies, the Burgundians, possessed most of northern France. It was then that the teenage girl heard heavenly voices urging her to take up arms and save her country. She became a soldier, inspired the French army; led the troops as they raised an English siege of Orléans; and in less than two years liberated a portion of France. But she was later taken prisoner and betrayed to the English, who had her declared a heretic and burned at the stake in 1431. In 1920, Joan was canonized as a saint by the Roman Catholic Church in admission that it had erred.

SUGGESTED READINGS

Best, Charles A. *Bernard Shaw and the Art of Drama*. Urbana: University of Illinois Press, 1973.
Gordon, David J. *Bernard Shaw and the Comic Divine*. New York: St. Martin's, 1990.
Holroyd, Michael. *Bernard Shaw*. New York: Random House, 1988.
Shaw, George Bernard. *Saint Joan*. East Rutherford, N.J.: Penguin, 2001.

3

Sean O'Casey
Juno and the Paycock
1924

After John Millington Synge, the next world-renowned dramatist to arise
from the Irish theater was Sean O'Casey (1880–1964), whose three tragicomedies, *The Shadow of a Gunman,* (1923), *Juno and the Paycock* (1924),
and *The Plough and the Stars* (1926), centered on the then-recent events of
Ireland's Easter Rebellion, War of Independence, and Civil War. They are
set in the Dublin tenements he knew well, and they turned the Irish theater
for a while toward bitter social criticism with O'Casey's dark thesis that the
acclaimed and glorified birth of the Irish nation was accompanied by deep
suffering, powerlessness, and tragedy for the little-regarded common people
who had been swept up in the raging torrent of history.

O'Casey was a self-taught playwright. He came to his art by seeing
plays in Dublin and by reading playwrights such as Ibsen, Strindberg, and
Shakespeare. He also read the plays of the most popular Irish dramatist of the
nineteenth century, the Dublin-born Dion Boucicault, a good craftsperson
from whom to learn dramatic structure.

O'Casey is the playwright of the poor and fragile inner-city families that
in the end have only love and a little dignity, and even they cannot be
counted on. O'Casey's ear for the dialect of the Dublin tenements was well
attuned; he had heard enough of it. Like Synge, he added a lyric quality to
his dialogue, and in so doing, he endowed his working-class characters with
a degree of respect.

O'Casey created delightfully humorous characterizations and some of the
most hilariously comic scenes in modern drama. There is a great love for
and understanding of humanity in this O'Casey, for his tenement people

represent all the common people of this sad, frightened, and very frightening world we live in.

Oddly, *Juno and the Paycock* and the other plays of the Dublin trilogy—so full of compassion for the poor of Dublin—initially were greeted with anger and derision by many members of the early audiences, in part because they felt that showing the poor as they were cast a bad light on Ireland and because O'Casey, a socialist and a pacifist, saw little value in any war, even a war of independence. But after initial disapproval, Irish audiences and then theater audiences throughout the English-speaking world, recognized that O'Casey had given Ireland three brilliant plays, the finest of which is *Juno and the Paycock*.

BIOGRAPHICAL CONTEXT

Sean O'Casey (1880–1964) was born John Casey, the youngest of eight children in a lower-middle-class Dublin Protestant family that sank to working-class status after the early death of the father, Michael Casey, when O'Casey was three years old. Overcrowded Dublin was an unhealthy place for children in the late nineteenth century, and three of O'Casey's seven siblings died in childhood. He himself was sickly and troubled with lifelong vision problems that may have been caused by malnutrition and unsanitary conditions that prevented him from obtaining more than a cursory elementary education.

When still a boy, O'Casey found employment as a laborer. At night, he pursued his religious and political interests in his local church; the Orange Lodge; the Gaelic League, where he studied Irish and began to call himself Sean O'Casey; the Irish Republican Brotherhood; and the Irish Citizen's Army, the political and militant arm of the Irish Transport and General Workers' Union. But one by one, these organizations disappointed him, and, disgruntled, he shed them all. O'Casey turned to books. He read English authors like Shakespeare, Shelley, and Dickens. He also admired the early plays of his fellow Dubliner Shaw.

Self-taught, O'Casey began writing journalism, history, poetry, and even greeting card verses for a Dublin publisher. Eventually, he came to dramatic writing in his forties after realizing that he could make use of his lifetime of observing Dublin tenement life to provide authentic dialogue and situations for plays. He also had a political agenda: socialism, not nationalism, could be the salvation of the proletariat.

In 1923, O'Casey offered a two-act play, *On the Run*, to Dublin's Abbey Theatre. Lady Augusta Gregory, the Abbey's comanager, was enthusiastic.

It was put on at the season's end as *The Shadow of a Gunman*. The play is set in a Dublin tenement as the War of Independence (1919–1921) is raging. In it, Minnie Powell, a young working-class woman living in a tenement, bravely removes bombs left in a room by a rebel and in doing so saves the life of a not-very-courageous young Irishman, Donal Davoren, who has pretended to be a fighter. But Minnie is shot by British irregulars—the notorious Black and Tans. And so the young man lives on in shame and ignominy. O'Casey embraced this antiwar position and, in *The Plough and the Stars*, applied it to the heroics of the Easter 1916 Rising, which in his view led to the wasted blood of the later War of Independence and the very dirty Irish Civil War.

Significantly, tenement life in Dublin had its first fully effective dramatic portrayal in *The Shadow of a Gunman*, though other writers had tried to portray the lives of the Dublin poor with little success. *Juno and the Paycock* (1924) and *The Plough and the Stars* (1926) quickly followed *The Shadow of a Gunman*. The pageant-like *The Plough and the Stars* is set at the time of the abortive Easter 1916 Rising. The play is drawn on a much larger scale than the preceding pieces in the Dublin trilogy. It is the story of ordinary people caught up in political events that are far beyond their control. The title comes from the symbols on the flag of the Irish Transport and General Workers' Union, of which O'Casey was once a member. That flag was one of those present at the Easter Rising because it was also carried by the Irish Citizen Army. It reflected O'Casey's worker background and identification with his lifelong socialism.

The Plough and the Stars brings several more inhabitants of a Dublin tenement to life. Most important are a young couple, Nora and Jack Clitheroe, who are expecting a child. It is Easter 1916. He is to be a commandant in the Citizen Army that will fight the British. She attempts to dissuade him from accepting the post but fails as he places honor and patriotism over family. Of course, he is killed, and Nora loses the baby and her mind.

Other characters are also memorable, especially the ever-talking Fluther Good and the alcoholic Protestant evangelist Bessie Burgess, who dies heroically when she is cut down by a stray bullet while shielding Nora. Always for O'Casey, the real heroes, the people with the greatest courage, are those whose instinctive sympathy and compassion cause them to act kindly, generously, and—most of all—unselfishly.

Nationalism and nationalist organizations are satirized by rowdy scenes in a pub, looting during the Rising, and a scalding indictment of the rebellion by the prostitute Rosie Redmond. In the end, while many of the inhabitants of the tenement are cowering in a room, the city is burning, Irish and British combatants are lying dead, and the surviving rebels are led away to prison as two British soldiers ironically sing, "Keep the Home Fires Burning."

The antiwar, antinationalist play was greeted with hostility by the audience and brought riots once more to the Abbey. An Irish writer was seen to be ridiculing Irish patriotism, nationalism, and the Irish character. The great Irish poet William Butler Yeats, the comanager of the Abbey Theatre, faced the incensed playgoers from the stage with a speech in which, alluding to the *Playboy of the Western World* riots, he said, "You have disgraced yourselves again!" But O'Casey's first three Abbey plays, often referred to as the Dublin trilogy, are O'Casey's greatest and most lasting achievement.

O'Casey's next play, an experimental, expensive-to-mount drama on World War I, *The Silver Tassie* (1928), was, to his surprise and chagrin, rejected by the Abbey. Yeats was ungracious and ungenerous this time. He did not like modernist dramas and World War I subjects. In addition, however, *The Silver Tassie* is flawed in that minor characters are two-dimensional and the language, unlike the dialogue in the Dublin trilogy, is devoid of sparkle.

The "tassie" is a silver cup awarded to a star football (soccer) player, Harry Heegan, in his illustrious days before a battle in World War I left him a cripple. In the first act, we see him in his athletic glory. Act 2 shows Harry in the battle in which he is badly wounded. In acts 3 and 4, he is in his wheelchair, paralyzed. At a dance he cannot participate in, he destroys the silver tassie out of frustration and anger.

The second act, set on the battlefield of northern France, is a powerful piece of expressionist-surrealist theater and a brilliant visual poem of despair, but it does not fit in stylistically with the rest of the drama. Finally, O'Casey let his powerful ideas overcome his dramaturgical instincts, and thus the play became propaganda. O'Casey took *The Silver Tassie* to London, where he had received the Hawthornden Prize for *Juno and the Paycock* and where he had married an Irish actress, Eileen Carey, who performed in London productions of his plays. He never returned to Ireland.

In the 1920s and early 1930s, O'Casey's antiwar and antinationalism dramas had considerable theatrical impact because their antiheroic stance perfectly caught the mood of most Western nations as their populations refuted the war fever and mindless chauvinism that had tumbled Europe into self-destruction from 1914 to 1918.

Living in Britain, O'Casey wrote a great many plays after *The Silver Tassie*—fantasies, expressionist dramas, and morality plays—but he never again wrote a play that was a popular and critical success. Several of his later plays and his autobiographies reflect his commitment to socialism and communism. Moreover, O'Casey's sharp tongue, short temper, tactlessness, and critical nature alienated many in the theater world.

Today, however, of the Irish playwrights who came into prominence during the tenure of Lady Gregory, Yeats, and Synge at the Abbey, O'Casey is the most frequently performed in Ireland and on the world stage. The Irish playwright who most learned from the early O'Casey was his fellow Dubliner Brendan Behan (1923–1964), who appreciated O'Casey's work with the Dublin dialect they shared, his efforts to show the truth of the lives of the urban poor, and his desire to portray their lives with dignity. In his two most important plays, *The Quare Fellow* (1954) and *The Hostage* (1958), Behan employed the O'Casey technique of blending humor, pathos, and tragedy while creating strong working-class Irish characters.

PLOT DEVELOPMENT

Juno and the Paycock is a play about the suffering of the poor and the way their lives are wasted. But it is also about human greatness achieved in the face of disaster, grief, and near hopelessness. Thus, the story, set in a Dublin tenement flat inhabited by the Boyle family, is a tragicomedy. "Captain" Jack Boyle is the "paycock (peacock)," who detests work and who lies, brags, and prefers boozing to all other activities. His sidekick is the parasitic Joxer Daly. They are a team, like a harmful Laurel and Hardy, and they have their theatrical ancestry in the bragging soldier and the wily slave of the Roman comedy of Plautus titled *Miles Glorious*.

Jack's wife, Juno, is a magnificent woman, a rock to whom all the members of a collapsing family cling. She is compassionate and courageous. Her lot is sad, even tragic, but she knows what is right and who is worth saving.

Juno and Jack Boyle have two grown children—hard-luck children. Johnny had been wounded—shot in the hip—as a rebel in the War for Independence, but after the peace treaty he joined the Irish Republican Army guerrilla diehards fighting the independent Irish government, and in that campaign he lost an arm. As *Juno and the Paycock* opens, Johnny is crippled, in pain, and now frightened because he has betrayed a rebel comrade. Later, rebel gunmen will come for the traitor, and he is executed offstage.

As the play opens, Juno and Mary Boyle, Jack and Juno's daughter, are talking about Robbie Tancred, a Republican guerrilla who has been assassinated. Johnny leaves the living room angered by what he sees as the women's insensitivity. Mary is on strike, and Juno scolds Mary for joining in when the family needs food, but Mary defends her actions as a matter of principle.

But Juno does not believe in causes, be they nationalistic or socialistic. Working people can't afford them. Mary's boyfriend, Jerry Devine, a labor leader, comes in to tell the women that Father Farrell has found a job for Jack, but this is not good news for the perennial malingerer.

Jack and Joxer, Boyle's sycophantic buddy, have come into the Boyle flat from their morning visit to the nearby pub. They are tipsy and full of song. Juno berates her lazy husband, who complains that he is unable to work because of the supposed pains in his legs. It is now Juno who must go out and work to support the entire family.

A schoolteacher and amateur lawyer, Jeremy Bentham, fatefully comes into the life of the Boyles. He announces that Jack Boyle has come into an inheritance of 2,000 pounds from a deceased cousin, and the family, especially Jack, goes on a spending spree, borrowing money while waiting for the bequest. It does not come because Bentham had erred in writing up the particulars of the will. Boyle now has creditors breathing down his neck and reclaiming his foolish and extravagant purchases. The family is financially ruined. Meanwhile, Mary had cooled her relationship with Jerry Devine and fallen for Bentham, but he has made her pregnant and cravenly run off to England. Jerry returns to propose to Mary again. He can forgive her affair with another man, but the news that she is pregnant with another man's child is too much for him, and he backs off. Even the best of Irish men is found wanting.

A drunken Boyle reviles Mary and wants to beat her, but Juno will not allow it. The compassionate Juno comforts her daughter and provides practical support. When she also learns that her son has been taken away and executed, she cries out to God and gathers up Mary as they leave to identify Johnny's body and find a new home for themselves. The intoxicated buddies, Jack and Joxer, hold the stage, oblivious to the tragedy about them as the curtain falls. Their comic banter is one of the pleasures of the play, although they contribute to "the terrible state o' chassis (chaos)" in their society. The family is destroyed, but the audience assumes that Juno, Mary, and the baby will endure and survive, for it is matriarchy, charged with the power of love, that sustains and preserves the human race.

CHARACTER DEVELOPMENT

"Captain" Jack Boyle, although amusing in action, is an irresponsible, lazy, lying, easily manipulated person. He is a poor husband and father, and he is a drunkard. In making Boyle such an extreme character, O'Casey satirizes all that could possibly be wrong with some working-class Irish men. Jack and Joxer are funny, of course, but a dark truth lies under the surface of the humor: impoverished Irish men, burdened with family, repress or ignore the stark realities of their sad lives through blustering belligerence, fantasizing, and mind-numbing intoxication.

Juno Boyle is one of the great female characters of Irish drama. She stands for all the suffering of Irish womanhood. She is the epitome of Irish mother-hood. Unlike the men in the play, Juno is neither political nor ideological. She is a pragmatic, compassionate human being who sees that no "ism" is of value to workers if they must have their bodies broken or their lives taken in its service. Juno grows in the course of the play. At first, she is not especially concerned when a neighbor's son is killed during the fratricidal warfare, but when she faces the death of her own son, she realizes that all mothers are losers in the masculinist struggles that consume young men. When her preg-nant daughter is threatened, she gives up her home to nurture and protect Mary and the grandchild to come. It is no accident that O'Casey gives Juno the name of the Roman queen of heaven.

Johnny Boyle, Jack and Juno's son, is both a disagreeable character and a victim to be pitied. He has given his health and sacrificed his future for the most radical version of the Irish nationalism: the Irish Republican Army. As a working-class youth, he had nothing to gain by fighting for Irish independence from Britain or against the new Free State government because no one cared about the welfare of the poor workers. Johnny's wiser mother knew that a worker's best "principle" is his ability to work.

Mary Boyle, Jack and Juno's daughter, is a more sympathetic character than her brother. She has fought for workers' rights and has been seduced and abandoned by a middle-class philanderer.

Jerry Devine, a labor leader and Mary's suitor, at first seems to redeem Irish manhood. He tries to get Boyle a job; he appears to love Mary even after she has jilted him for smooth-talking Bentham. Jerry offers to marry her despite that fact. The audience is silently cheering him when O'Casey smashes our hopes for Mary by having Devine do a quick about-face when he learns that Mary is pregnant with his rival's child. Devine is not divine after all.

THEMES

A main theme of *Juno and the Paycock* is O'Casey's attack on nationalist ideology. As a socialist, O'Casey is much more interested in the problems of the working class than he is concerned for who is ruling Ireland. The crippled and terrified Johnny, soon to be executed as a traitor by the very same men he soldiered with, is O'Casey's symbol for what he saw as the foolish waste of life that both the Irish War of Independence and the Irish Civil War brought about. O'Casey parodies Irish nationalism when he has Jack Boyle vainly try to run his household in the style of a British monarch as he plans to make Juno take an oath of allegiance to him.

The arrogance, egoism, and insensitivity of Irish men fuel another important theme in *Juno and the Paycock*: the cost of patriarchy to Irish women. O'Casey implies that masculine vanity and shiftlessness—along with love of drink—are the curses on Irish womanhood.

NARRATIVE STYLE

O'Casey's diction in *Juno and the Paycock* is informal, colloquial, and a replication of the pronunciation, syntax, and vocabulary of inner Dublin of the early decades of the twentieth century. Surprisingly, the fact that a great many of the speeches in the play are relatively long and thus seemingly not conversational does not hinder the smooth flow of dialogue and the credibility of characterization. O'Casey's working-class characters, through speech and action, weave a sustained texture of realism that is successfully maintained throughout the play. O'Casey adds a timeless epic quality to the portraits of Juno and the Captain—as if they are neoclassical prototypes. Simultaneously, Juno's development in the play from indifferent homemaker to determined protector of her daughter and the child to come is a powerful romantic construction of a great character.

HISTORICAL CONTEXT

Juno and the Paycock, produced in 1924, is set in 1922 in Dublin, when a brutal civil war blazed between the new Irish government, which had successfully liberated 26 of the 32 counties of Ireland, and those former freedom fighters who had opposed the signing of the December 1921 peace treaty with Great Britain that had created the Irish Free State. Those Republicans, angry because the new country did not include the six counties of Ulster, engaged in guerilla warfare on their former comrades-in-arms. In the play, O'Casey calls them diehards. In 1923, they had been decisively defeated and scattered, but even as the play was first being performed, a few small pockets of rebels were still resisting the government whose authority had been legalized by a majority of the Irish people in a referendum.

SUGGESTED READINGS

Krause, David. *Sean O'Casey: The Man and His Work*. Rev. ed. New York: Macmillan, 1975.

Murray, Christopher. *Sean O'Casey: Artist at Work*. Dublin: Gill and Macmillan, 2005.

O'Casey, Sean. *Juno and the Paycock*. In *Three Dublin Plays*. London: Faber and Faber, 2000.

4

Noël Coward
Private Lives
1930

Noël Coward was the consummate theater person. He could write, compose music, act, sing, dance, direct, and design. He was suave, adroit, and graceful. Coward was creativity personified. Between the two world wars, no other playwright was as uniformly successful as he was. Indeed, Noël Coward was the ultimate theatrical personage of the twentieth century. *Private Lives* is Coward's finest play. From its first London West End run, the play was seen to epitomize the gaiety, frivolity, and irreverence of the 1920s. A perennial favorite around the world, it is constantly revived, and its durability is astounding. Its wit and satire are worthy of, indeed indebted to, Oscar Wilde.

Coward's plays show a certain indifference to the problems of the world. Upper-class privilege lives on in plays like *Private Lives* long after the world came to think it bad taste to flaunt it. His flashy, sardonic world was never real—theater is not life after all—but by suspending disbelief for three hours, an audience believes it and enjoys the smart set's indifference to the middle class and smirking contempt for anyone not one of them.

BIOGRAPHICAL CONTEXT

Noël Coward (1899–1973) wrote more than 60 comedies of manners, farces, historical dramas, musicals, and revues. Sophisticated, witty, suave, and outwardly very sure of himself, he was also a gay man who suffered much of his life because his image as a romantic leading man in his seemingly heterosexual comedies and the many love songs he composed required him to keep his sexual life a secret to the general public, if not to his friends and colleagues in the theater. Onstage, Coward's high camp was accepted by the audience as straight. Thus, Coward, who became Sir Noël Coward when he was knighted shortly before his death, was an establishment figure who was secretly antiestablishment. Many commentators have noted that Coward's carefully crafted public image of an elegant upper-class personage, full of poise, and brilliant in quotable cocktail conversation was his most successful artistic creation.

Noël Pierce Coward was born in Teddington, a London suburb, to poor parents with connections to gentry. His father was a piano salesman who barely made enough money to support his family. His mother, who took in lodgers to help financially, strongly encouraged her son to have a theatrical career. Both Coward parents were musical, and the stage seemed the best opportunity for a bright and precocious child. Coward's formal education was limited. He attended Chapel Royal School in Clapham and took dancing lessons. His acting career began at the tender age of 11 in a Christmas play performed at London's famous exposition center, the Crystal Palace. At the age of 14, he played a minor role in James M. Barrie's *Peter Pan*.

Early fame came to Coward in 1917 with his play *Vortex*, about a well-born young drug addict who finds his mother's adulterous behavior impossible to bear and so forces her to confront the reality of her existence as he gives up his habit. The next year, he was conscripted into the British army as World War I was winding down. Assigned for training to the Artists' Rifles, he was soon declared unfit for military service and returned to civilian life.

Coward's early stage successes include the outrageous *Fallen Angels* (1925), in which two women make a date with a lover they shared before they embarked on their present dull marriages, and when he does not show, they settle for getting drunk; *Hay Fever* (1925), a madcap comedy about the eccentric, theatrical, and self-centered Bliss family; and *Bitter Sweet* (1929), a nostalgic operetta that introduced such favorite romantic songs as "I'll See You Again" and "If Love Were All."

Private Lives (1930) is a near perfect comedy about falling in love a second time with one's first spouse; *Design for Living* (1933) portrays a happy ménage à trois; *Blithe Spirit* (1941) has the ghost of a deceased first wife exorcised so that the hero and his second wife can live happily ever after. *Present Laughter* (1943) is about an actor who struts like a peacock and who maintains an unconventional household with the help of his former wife, whose true worth he realizes in the end.

Coward often performed in his own plays, especially in the earlier part of his life. His London successes generally were replicated on Broadway.

Coward loved to travel. America and the Far East were favorite destinations for him prior to World War II.

Coward the patriot wrote *Cavalcade* (1931), a large-cast panorama of British life from 1899 (the year of his birth and the beginning of the Boer War) to 1930, through the history of the Marryot family and their servants, the Bridges. Today, however, the play seems a class-bound, chauvinistic spectacle.

Just before the beginning of World War II, Coward wrote the patriotic *This Happy Breed* (1939), an appreciation of his proud English heritage. During World War II, Coward served his country as an entertainer of troops, performing in Britain, the United States, Canada, and other allied countries. During the war, he wrote, produced, and acted in the film *In Which We Serve* (1942), in which a valiantly manned British destroyer is sunk in the Mediterranean Sea.

After World War II, Coward was more popular with American audiences than he was with British audiences. But eventually for both, Coward's plays seemed slight and out of date. Audiences weaned on less sophisticated musicals and more naturalistic dramas did not catch the subtlety and satire in his plays and saw them as too superficial. But many of his comedies and musicals are still produced, his songs are still sung, and the film *Brief Encounters* (1944), for which he wrote the screenplay (he wrote several successful screenplays), remains a romantic classic of the British cinema. Today, repertory companies find that producing certain of Coward's plays provides exhilaration in audiences and casts through nostalgia for a lost world that seemed more carefree and simpler than our own.

Coward built a house in Jamaica and lived there and in Switzerland from the 1950s until his death in 1973. Coward received many awards and accolades culminating in being elected a Fellow of the Royal Society of Literature in 1970 and being knighted the same year.

PLOT DEVELOPMENT

With its brilliant dialogue and titillating plot, *Private Lives*, a comedy of manners, is a satire on the thrill-seeking and marriage-go-round of upper-class British society in the Flapper Age, the 1920s. The frequently revived comedy often serves as a star turn for a celebrity acting couple playing the parts of Amanda and Elyot and enjoying a cathartic marital battle nightly on the stage.

The plot features a high-society couple, Amanda and Elyot. They have divorced, and, as the curtain rises, they have found new spouses and are on their respective honeymoons. As chance—or Noël Coward—would have it, both couples have just checked into adjoining rooms at a high-class hotel at a French seaside resort. The rooms actually have adjoining balconies. Elyot Chase's bride, Sybil, is young and insecure with her older, more sophisticated and experienced husband. Amanda's new husband, Victor Prynne, is pompous, humorless, and gullible.

Unaware of the presence of their former mates, Amanda and Elyot come out on the balcony in the early evening to enjoy the romantic view of the harbor. Separately, each sees the ex-spouse, and each immediately wants to move out of the hotel before their spouses learn of the next-door neighbors. But the spouses, even after learning of the presence of their predecessors, do not wish to leave.

Meanwhile, Elyot and Amanda are mesmerized by the beauty of the harbor scene and the mellifluous sound of the hotel orchestra. Elyot remarks, "Extraordinary how potent cheap music is." They realize that they still love each other even after five years of separation, while their new mates seem less attractive after just hours of married life. So, leaving their new spouses behind, Amanda and Elyot run off to Paris together.

Act 2 takes place in Amanda's Paris flat. At first, there is peace between Elyot and her, but they soon return to their old love–hate relationship. Elyot is annoyed that Amanda had several affairs before remarrying, but he cannot understand why Amanda is bothered by the fact that he had affairs too. After agreeing to divorce their current spouses and remarrying, they fall into jealous tantrums and a spectacular fight. The fight scene is the high point of the farce. Exhausted, each combatant then retreats to a separate bedroom, not noticing that Sybil and Victor quietly have entered the room. The aggrieved parties must spend the night draped on separate pieces of uncomfortable furniture.

Act 3 is morning. Victor and Sybil blame each other's mate for the trouble. When all four are in the room together, Victor wants to beat up Elyot, who sanely refuses to participate in such a cliché act. While Sybil and Victor begin to quarrel over fault—just as if they were married—and Sybil slaps Victor, Amanda and Elyot, now bemused observers, slip away to renew their life together.

CHARACTER DEVELOPMENT

Amanda, Elyot, Sybil, and Victor are highly individualized representatives of the most affluent class in between-the-wars British society. In a way, they are descendents of Oscar Wilde's Victorian lovers in *The Importance of Being Earnest*. None of the wealthy upper-class lovers in Wilde's play or *Private Lives* have any work to do. They are the parasitic, idle rich who devote their youthful and not-so-youthful days to amour. They simply assume that they have every right to their lunacies and pleasures as long as they live their lives with style. The blind egotism of Amanda and Elyot provokes laughter and a shaking of the head. The frenetic nature of their relationship is delightfully farcical if somewhat sad, for in the end we realize that they will never have peace.

Amanda, in her early thirties, is an attractive sophisticated woman. Makeup and haute couture are part of the package. Additionally, her wit and her daring make her especially desirable to men of her class (the only ones she would be interested in), and she has had her share of them. But as far as the heart is concerned, Amanda has loved only Elyot.

Elyot is 35 or so, handsome, sophisticated, wealthy, well educated, and a rather jaded roué. Having had affairs with several women close to his own age after a disastrous marriage with Amanda, he had decided to settle down again. As a precaution against committing to a mature and liberated woman who could match his wit, he has married a woman a dozen years younger than he is. Elyot would not have been happy with Sybil even if he had not run into his one true love on the hotel balcony on the night of his second honeymoon.

Sybil is a childish, spoiled, demanding, young woman who thinks that a husband is a man who can be molded to her specifications. She has married out of her league if not her class. Sybil thinks that a wife's tears is the spur to move a husband in the direction she wants him to go. By refusing to leave the hotel when Elyot has pointed out the difficulty, if not the danger, of staying in the same hotel with his ex-wife and new husband, Sybil sealed her fate. Elyot and Sybil could never be happy with each other.

Victor is a brusque, cocky, not-too-bright, insensitive, bullying man in his early thirties. He seems such an unlikely choice as a husband for Amanda that surely Amanda must have been bored with the dating game and ready to settle for a stable suitor who would provide security. Victor will never be passionate about a woman. His intransigence in not wanting to leave the hotel when Amanda has told him of Elyot's presence and the situation in the hotel is a fatal act of what the ancient Greeks called hubris. He is left at war with Sybil, with whom he may make a miserable marriage someday. Who knows or cares?

THEMES

In *Private Lives*, Coward argues that society has no real hold on individual lives. He subverts moral standards about sex and fidelity in marriage. In fact,

Coward's plays often center on the exchange of partners. This was quite shocking to middle-class audiences even as late as the mid-twentieth century. Of course, *Private Lives* seemed particularly and deliciously wicked in that the leading couple changed partners twice. Thus, marriage for Coward is not a sacrament but a contract between lovers who are required to remain faithful only as long as each spouse is amorous and interesting.

Coward upends the conventions of romantic comedy, in which eligible couples, seemingly destined for each other, overcome impediments and marry. In *Private Lives*, the sanctity of marriage is mocked, and eligibility gives way to passion without cost to the lovers. Coward does embrace the romantic concept that love can afflict anyone. But in the case of Amanda and Elyot, the lovers are as incapable of living together as apart.

In *Private Lives*, Coward valorizes urbanity. It pervades the play. The life worth living is one within the privileged social set: affording splendid digs, first-class travel, having fun, selfish indulgence, snubbing "inferiors," misbehaving, gossiping, and putting down friends. One cannot imagine Amanda and Elyot as parents: poor kids!

NARRATIVE STYLE

Coward preferred comedy to tragicomedy or tragedy. He wanted his audience to laugh and to feel good at the end of a play. Farce was the perfect style for him. Farce relies to a large extent on physical comedy, and there is much of that in *Private Lives*, especially in the scenes set in the Paris flat. Farce also employs an improbable plot. The plot of *Private Lives* is just that, with the coincidence of the honeymooners checking in to the same hotel at the same time and having adjoining rooms with an adjoining balcony. Farce is usually about characters exhibiting seemingly bad behavior. In *Private Lives*, Amanda and Elyot go all the way, so to speak. They are really behaving immorally. Thus, the play was outrageously dangerous at the time it was produced and escaped censorship only because it was comedy and contained no profanity.

The snappy, short-line, staccato dialogue in *Private Lives* is a fountain of trivia. In the conversation of the smart set, what is said is less important than how it is said. Form wins over content. Elyot and Amanda are master and mistress of small talk that is full of non sequiturs, inanities, and gossip. They joust and posture and consider the effect of their witticisms on their antagonist. They are people who simply assume that because they are witty, clever, good looking, glamorous, or rich, they do not have to live according to the morality of the majority. Coward is satirizing them, of course, but as

Private Lives is a romantic comedy of manners and not a dark comedy of vice, the author goes easy on two characters he liked so much. Significantly, in the initial run of the play, he played Elyot, and his lifelong friend, the actress Gertrude Lawrence, played Amanda.

HISTORICAL CONTEXT

Private Lives seemed a model of daring to the post–World War I British generation. The nation had turned inward after the war, tired of conflict in Europe, conflict in the empire, and labor-management and class conflict at home, especially during the General Strike of 1926. Coward's title for his masterpiece perfectly stated what the audience was interested in: private lives—not politics or social problems.

Elyot Chase, the play's hero, at about 30 years old in 1930, would have been 18 when World War I ended. (Coward was 19 when called for service and sent home as unfit.) Elyot would have just missed conscription and a trip to France to be shot at and perhaps killed or mutilated in the trenches. He would have learned of the deaths of a great many slightly older schoolmates and relatives. Elyot's pursuit of pleasure and madcap behavior is that of someone who narrowly escaped death and who sees his life as a gift.

SUGGESTED READINGS

Coward, Noël. *Private Lives*. London: Methuen, 2002.
Hoare, Philip. *Noël Coward*. London: Mandarin, 1996.
Levin, Milton. *Noël Coward*. Boston: Twayne, 1989.

5

Samuel Beckett
Waiting for Godot
1953

In *Waiting for Godot,* a great writer saw the condition of humankind through a glass darkly and translated that vision to the stage. *Waiting for Godot* is the great twentieth-century play of inquiring, of skeptical seeking for a meaning to life, and of questioning not the existence of God but the existence of existence.

Waiting for Godot is a play without the usual elements of obvious plot and progressive narration. It exists in a timeless scene and almost in a timeless world. The characters are human beings waiting in vain for revelation. They, like all humans, continue to wait, to hope, and to expect while trying to maintain some semblance of dignity, some communication with others, and some concern for those with whom their lives are linked. And when all is said and done, we hope we shall be able to say, like Vladimir, that at least we have kept our appointments.

Beckett sees the modern artist as someone in a bind because there is nothing really to express, nor is there a true desire to express nothingness. Yet the artist must do his or her work, which, paradoxically, is to express. Meanwhile, living is suffering, hope is cruel, and existence may be nauseating, but the wisdom from such realizations may be what makes life bearable.

BIOGRAPHICAL CONTEXT

Samuel Barclay Beckett (1906–1989) was born into an affluent Protestant family of mercantile Huguenot origins, in Foxrock, one of Dublin's fashionable suburbs south of the city. He was the second son and last child of William

Beckett, a successful cost estimator and materials facilitator in the building industry; and the former Maria (May) Jones Roe, who had nursed in the hospital in which William Beckett was briefly a patient. From the beginning, Samuel was called Sam.

Sam's elementary schooling from age five to nine was at the Misses Elsners' Academy near Foxrock. There he began an intense study of French that continued throughout his formal education. From ages nine through 13, he was a commuter student at the Earlsfort School in Dublin. In 1920, he was sent north to study at the Eton-like Portora Royal School in Enniskillen, County Fermanagh, and then he entered Trinity College, Dublin, majoring in modern languages. He was graduated with a B.A. in 1927, and he accepted a position teaching French in Belfast at Campbell College, a prestigious public (private) school. Although he later returned to Trinity College as a lecturer in French and subscribed for his M.A. in 1931, Beckett intensely disliked teaching.

In 1928, Beckett went to Paris to work as a lecturer in the Ecole Normale Supérieure. In the French capital, which in the Jazz Age was the avant-garde capital of Western culture, he met and was befriended by James Joyce, who became his mentor. Beckett helped Joyce, whose eyesight was failing, as a reader, and he occasionally took dictation and did research. Unfortunately, Joyce's mentally disturbed daughter, Lucia, fell in love with Beckett, and his rejection of her added to her difficulties. The Joyce family felt that Beckett had led Lucia on, which he had not, but cordial relations between the Joyces and the young writer were broken off for a time. Nevertheless, James Joyce would always remain the greatest linguistic influence on the younger author.

At this time, Beckett began to publish in periodicals, and then in 1930 his long poem *Whorescope* was published between covers, followed by *Proust* (1931), a critical study. Returning to Ireland in 1931, Beckett taught French at Trinity College, hoping to please his family with a conventional job, but he still hated teaching, and so he walked out on the lectureship and promptly fled back to Paris to escape Trinity and his pious and difficult mother, with whom he had a love–hate relationship. His visits to Ireland were always traumatic to the sensitive writer.

In 1932, he returned home again, ill and destitute, to obtain medical treatment and to write. Now he consciously eschewed realism in his creative writing. The next year, his beloved and generous father died unexpectedly, leaving Beckett a small inheritance. Fortunately, Beckett's collection of comic stories, *More Pricks Than Kicks* (1934), was accepted by Chatto and Windus, his first significant publication in fiction. The chronically depressed young writer, wracked with psychosomatic illnesses, received psychoanalytic treatment in London from 1933 to 1935 from Carl Jung, whose lectures he also attended. Additionally, Beckett read extensively in psychology.

The years up through 1937, when he was writing *Murphy* (1938), his first published novel, were peripatetic ones for Beckett as he moved back and forth in continual ill health between London and the family home, Cooldrinagh, in Foxrock. He also had an extended sojourn in Germany to study the language and contemporary painting (the painter Jack Yeats was one of his good friends) and to see what was happening to that nation under the repugnant Nazis. After a final break with his smothering mother in 1937, Beckett moved to Paris, the city that he would make his home for the remainder of his life.

In 1938, Beckett was stabbed by a mugger on a Paris street, and a young piano student, Suzanne Deschevaux-Dumesnil, visited him in the hospital. Beckett and Suzanne became lovers and lifelong partners. They finally married in 1961.

When France was overrun by the Germans in World War II, Beckett committed himself to France, although Eire was neutral, and he courageously joined the French Resistance in 1941. Betrayed along with others in his Resistance unit, he and Suzanne had to flee Paris to hide from the Gestapo in the village of Roussillon, in the Vaucluse, about 30 miles from Avignon, laboring through 1944 as agricultural workers and helping the Resistance until U.S. troops liberated the village. In 1945, he joined the staff of the Irish Red Cross hospital at Saint Lô. For his services to France, he was awarded the Croix de Guerre and the Médaille de la Reconnaissance after the war.

Beckett's major novels were either written in French and translated by himself into English or written in English and translated into French. The novels are *Murphy* (1938) noted previously, *Watt* (written during World War II and published in 1953), *Molloy* (1951), *The Unnamable* (1953), *Malone Dies* (1957), and *How It Is* (1961). All are philosophical works in which Beckett moves from logical positivism to deep, despairing existentialism. It is in Beckett's fiction that Joyce's influence is most apparent. But unlike Joyce, Beckett was a secularist, uninterested in myth. In that respect, he was more like another Parisian friend, the philosopher Jean Paul Sartre. They espoused phenomenology: All you get is what you experience through imperfect sensual perceptions. Nothing transcends the boundaries of human experience.

Waiting for Godot (1953) is Beckett's greatest drama, a profound statement on the human condition. It made history but slowly. It opened in Paris, performed in French as first written. Produced in English in London, it became a critical success. In the United States, it failed at first and then was recognized as the masterpiece it is. *Waiting for Godot* is a minimalist experimental play that influenced twentieth-century European and American drama more than any other drama, a play that seemed for a while to have ended realism on the stage and the conventions of the well-made play—exposition, complication, and resolution—and it was the work that led to Beckett's Nobel Prize for Literature in 1969.

Endgame, a one-act play, appeared in 1958, having first been written as *Fin de Partie* a year before. *Acte Sans Paroles* (1957), a mime play, became *Act without Words* (1958). The one-act dramatic monologue *Krapp's Last Tape* (1958) is one of Beckett's most frequently performed dramas. The ironically titled *Happy Days* appeared in 1961 and was the last of Beckett's major dramas, although he continued to write plays with diminishing dialogue and lessening action for 15 more years.

Beckett's plays are more theater than drama. The texts support and highlight performances. The plays are spectacular in the sense that the audience learns almost as much from looking as from listening. The actor's business in Beckett's dramas is often slapstick, the effect of the silent-film comedians, like Charley Chaplin and Buster Keaton, on his work. Vladimir and Estragon did not evolve far from Chaplin's "Little Tramp." The plays are vehicles for multiple "readings." Each member of the audience or each reader sees and/or feels the play individually as the archetypal scene washes over the senses and the simple but profound words register.

Except for occasional trips, after World War II Beckett spent the rest of his life in Paris and in a modest country cottage in Ussy, a village 40 miles from the city. Although he had turned down many honors, in 1959 he accepted an honorary Doctor of Letters Degree from Trinity. In 1961, he married Suzanne Deschevaux-Dumesnil in order to secure for her an inheritance. In 1969, he accepted the Nobel Prize for Literature but did not attend the award ceremony in Stockholm. He and his wife felt that the award was a disaster, as the notoriety impinged on his writing time and their privacy.

Beckett spent much of his later life directing productions of his plays in various European cities. His dramas were so much a product of his intense imagination that he was adamant in requiring that they be staged exactly as in the original staging. He also demanded exactitude in line readings. Beckett saw his dramas as fixed creations regardless of whether they were in text or performance.

As his fame grew, he became more and more reclusive and secretive. His friends tended more to be artists and theater people than writers and intellectuals.

From early manhood, Beckett drank copious amounts of Irish whisky and was a heavy smoker. In failing health, he moved into Le Tiers Temps, a nursing home. He died of emphysema and Parkinson's disease on December 22, 1989, in the Hôpital Saint-Anne. Up to the last few weeks of his life, Beckett continued to write. Suzanne had preceded Sam in death on July 17. He was buried next to her. They had no children.

PLOT DEVELOPMENT

Waiting for Godot is a minimalist tragicomedy that reduces human life to its fundamental pain and its few and small pleasures. Tragicomedy eschews the structure of tragedy, which emphasizes the nobility of the hero, the power of fate, and resolution in banishment or death. Tragicomedies alternate tragic and comic situations. In *Waiting for Godot,* waiting is the beginning and the end in itself, while the action is only process, not a means to an end.

In *Waiting for Godot,* the protagonists, two tramps, Vladimir and Estragon, have only their suffering to prove they are alive and only their fragile friendship to comfort them. Their world—and, by implication, the audience's world—is a nearly featureless landscape: a barren place except for its one, initially leafless, tree.

In act 1, the tramps are waiting for someone named Godot to rescue them from their misery. Estragon is struggling to pull off his too-tight boot. Vladimir informs his friend that he has spent the night in a ditch where he was beaten. To pass the time, the men talk about the Bible and the two thieves who were crucified with Christ. They consider hanging themselves from the one sad tree.

Godot does not come. The tramps are not even sure they are in the right place. Instead, a cruel, whip-wielding master, Pozzo, and his silent, demented former teacher and slave, Lucky, tethered on a long rope and burdened with baggage and a stool, arrive. They stay a short while so that Pozzo can smoke his pipe and talk about selling the sobbing Lucky. Sympathetically, Vladimir goes to wipe Lucky's tears with Pozzo's handkerchief and for his trouble gets a vicious kick in the shins from the silent one. Lucky is then forced to dance and then to think aloud. He makes a mad, jumbled, frenzied philosophical speech: the lecture of an insane professor. Finally, Pozzo and Lucky leave as they came—roped together.

The tramps return to waiting. At the end of the act, a messenger boy arrives, announcing, supposedly from Godot, that Godot will come tomorrow, then flees. Night falls suddenly while, swiftly and comically, the moon rises and climbs the sky. The tramps decide to go but do not.

Act 2 finds the tree showing five leaves, so time has passed, but how much? Supposedly, it is the next day. Vladimir enters and sings a children's song as Estragon shows up. They try to convince each other that they are happier together than when they are alone. To pass the time, they ask each other questions. The tramps continue the unending process of waiting. Estragon has forgotten yesterday's events until they discover that Estragon's shin is still bleeding where Lucky kicked him. They try to entertain themselves by playing Pozzo and Lucky.

Pozzo and Lucky return still tethered together and collapse. Now Pozzo is blind, and Lucky is mute again. The tramps help Pozzo up. Lucky will not take advantage of the situation to reverse roles. Pozzo makes a speech about the bitterness of life. Then he goads Lucky on, and they exit as they had entered.

The boy messenger arrives again. He claims not to be the one who came yesterday. His message is that Godot will come tomorrow. The boy is questioned about Godot to little avail, and he exits. The tramps try to hang themselves using the cord that is Estragon's belt, but they fail, and Estragon's trousers fall. With nightfall they decide to part and meet the next day to wait for Godot. Agreeing to leave, they stay as the tragicomedy ends.

It is for the audience to ask and answer its own questions, such as, Where are the tramps, and why are they there? What is their relationship? Who is Godot? Does he really exist? Is the messenger telling the truth? What is the meaning of the suddenly blooming tree? What is the significance of the Pozzo–Lucky relationship? Is there any resolution or closure to this stark play punctuated with black humor? Why can't they go? Why can't they let go?

Waiting for Godot is Beckett's chief vision of the inner universe, the human mind in the brief interval between the womb and the tomb. It is the end of hope. We wait with Vladimir and Estragon in hopeless hope for the play to end and for life to end. Waiting is the human condition. But if we are waiting in pain for something, someone, Godot or God, we are deceived. The existential credo is not the Cartesian "I think therefore I am"; it is the existential "I suffer therefore I am."

CHARACTER DEVELOPMENT

Estragon, who's nickname is Gogo, is of the earth. His name is French for "tarragon," an aromatic herb used as a seasoning in pickling. His obsession with his ill-fitting boots that cause him pain indicates that he is close to or of the earth. Gogo also goes and comes. He is the wanderer who always stumbles back to his companion Didi. He can be sarcastic and skeptical, but mostly he is resigned to an inevitably unhappy fate.

Vladimir, whose nickname is Didi, continually looks and feels into his hat, seeking cooties or some other irritant, just as Gogo is tormented by his ill-fitting boot. He is more rational and less emotional than Gogo. Vladimir seems more in touch with the outside world and more aware of his immediate world. He is better spoken than Gogo, and he sings in both acts. He is the leader of the pair, and, significantly, he is the one who most believes in Godot.

Estragon and Vladimir support each other. They are a small community, a society of two dedicated to ritualistic waiting—waiting for something sacred, something or someone new to their experience if not the world. In a sense, they are married. The dialogic passages of Estragon and Vladimir destroy language through the torrent of words. Their relationship contrasts with that of Pozzo and Lucky in that neither one is dominant. Surprisingly, when their nicknames are spoken together in quick succession, "Gogo and Didi" sounds close to "Godot." Together they are objects of pity because they cannot escape their fate or the play, and the implied ending of their lives has them still waiting and then separated forever by death.

Pozzo is a sadist, enjoying his power over his slave, Lucky, but he is also weary of the relationship. After all, a master is always tied to the slave who serves him. Pozzo and Lucky live on the road, coming and going. One is reminded of the legend of the Flying Dutchman, an evil sea captain condemned to sail the seas forever. Pozzo, in his selfishness and cruelty, personifies evil. Simultaneously, Pozzo stands for capitalism exploiting the worker, Lucky. The derby or bowler hat enforces this consideration. Pozzo is all materialism, concerned about his baggage, his comfort, his food, his pipe, and his watch. Lucky has nothing but his hat and his burdens.

Lucky is a slavish masochist who does not want relief from his pain and thus attacks Estragon. The fact that he does not take advantage of Pozzo's blindness in act 2 to escape or kill his enslaver indicates that he has need of the relationship and even the punishment. Lucky is not only a symbol of the exploited worker in a capitalist society but also the tormented intellectual made ineffectual by that society. It may be that Pozzo and Lucky are yin and yang in their relationship: part of one personality or entity.

Lucky's vomited tirade when he is compelled to think is like a mad academic lecture, full of phrases that seem to make sense but are linguistic islands. Beckett is saying, Do not trust language; it is only air, ink, or fleeting image.

The messenger is called "the Boy." He brings the information that Godot is not coming today, but is coming tomorrow. He is a goatherd, and he seems a character out of the Bible living a pastoral life. But there may be two messengers because the boy tells Vladimir in the second act that he has come for the first time. Godot may be his father or God the Father. Significantly, a child arrives each time just as the tramps are losing heart. In a sense, a boy-herder brings the men back to the fold. In Greek tragedy, the messenger brings information that leads to catastrophe and closure, but in *Waiting for Godot,* the messenger is only the medium for an enormous cosmic tease.

Perhaps Godot should be listed in the cast of characters. Beckett was asked more than once if Godot is God. His answer was that if he wanted Godot to be God, he would have called him God. Still, the hope of seeing Godot and being saved by Godot is what sustains Estragon and Vladimir, who are Christians concerned with the meaning and message of the Bible in their miserable existence. It may be that Godot does not exist (although the boy seems guileless), and Beckett, despite his pat answer, may be implying that God does not exist and thus that religion is a costly joke on humankind.

THEMES

Obviously, Beckett is a philosophical writer, and *Waiting for Godot* is a philosophical play. Under the influence of French and German existentialists, Beckett wants the audience to question all intangible values, such as belief in the existence of the Deity, patriotism, truth, love, friendship, honor, power, and even intellectual accomplishment. We must recognize that humans are cruel to each other. They exploit and betray even those closest to them.

Waiting for Godot is simultaneously about the need for identity and the loss of it. Existing in a blighted landscape, Vladimir and Estragon seem like survivors of a catastrophic tragedy: a nuclear war, genocide, a world-jarring volcanic eruption, or a meteor strike. They are humanity reduced to basics. That is the human condition. Beckett wants us to contemplate the smallness of our lives. Perhaps only some human companionship can assuage the pain of existence.

NARRATIVE STYLE

Aristotle, in *Poetics* (323 B.C.), states that plays need to have a beginning, a middle, and an end. *Waiting for Godot* has those parts only in the most literal sense. The two acts of the tragicomedy are similar. In both acts, Vladimir and Estragon appear and try to pass the time while waiting for Godot as required. Pozzo and Lucky appear and depart in both acts. The boy messenger appears and departs in both acts. Thus, rather than building from exposition through complications to a climax and then closure, the parts of the play simply replicate as if one day would be the same as the days in acts 1 and 2. Time and life itself are cyclical. Dawn comes, night falls, and the moon rises.

Thus, *Waiting for Godot* is purposely not very dramatic—as daily life is not very dramatic—but it is theatrical. The characters say poetic and philosophical things, they do amusing things, they inform the audience of their past and their relationships, they tell of their sufferings while sometimes inflicting pain on others, and they make us think about God, nature, and what it means to be a human being.

Beckett blends the natural and unnatural, the real and the absurd, and the poetic and dramatic with the verbal economy of a modern poem. One moment, Vladimir and Estragon or Pozzo are presenting philosophical statements directly to the audience, and the next moment the stage is filled with slapstick mayhem. In fact, Beckett chose drama as the genre for his greatest philosophical statement because it combines language and gesture. Thus, *Waiting for Godot* is both abstract and sensual. It is a play of ideas that are presented in ritual terms: repetitions, mysticism, and dialogue that can be chanted; religious symbols like a tree to be used for sacrifice as well as suicide; and a road for an epic journey, but one on which Vladimir and Estragon do not set out because they are pledged to waiting. Ironically, the road leads not to the Holy Grail or home but to nowhere. Anyway, Estragon and Vladimir are forced to stay where they are and in the play.

There is humor in *Waiting for Godot*. Vladimir and Estragon are dressed like Charlie Chaplin with his derby. Farcical elements are present: pants fall down, shoes are too large or too tight, hats are exchanged in a comic ballet, and kicks and tumbles occur. Beckett wanted his tragicomedy to be played for laughs, for laughter may be all that is left after total despair.

Beckett employs several theatrical traditions in *Waiting for Godot*. The circus and the music hall (vaudeville) are referred to. Clowns with derby hats remind the audience of the farcical qualities of the commedia dell'arte. Pantomime connects with British and Irish Christmas extravaganzas. The staccato verse form called stichomythia and the coming and going of a messenger reflect Greek classical plays, as does the choruslike direct address to the audience by Vladimir and Estragon.

The seriocomic ambiguity and puzzling symbolic word play of Godot was partly inspired by the dramaturgy of Eugéne Ionesco, Jean Genet, and Arthur Adamov while foreshadowing the plays of Tom Stoppard, Harold Pinter, Edward Albee, and others in the Theater of the Absurd.

Beckett is an existentialist writer, and *Waiting for Godot* is an existentialist drama. Existentialism, a philosophy founded in Europe in the middle of the twentieth century, states that individuals exist in an unfathomable universe, never knowing the ultimate consequence of their actions but, nevertheless, remaining responsible for those actions. All of us wait within the prison of our senses. We are really alone: that is the essential (or existential) fact of the human condition. Humankind, floating in futility and acting irrationally, never realizes the impossibility of real communication between individuals.

Ultimately, *Waiting for Godot* is a brilliant exercise in the use of ennui in the service of style. It testifies to the nothingness—which is the all—of existence.

HISTORICAL CONTEXT

Immediately after World War II ended, Beckett served with the Irish Red Cross in Normandy treating civilian and military casualties. Naturally, he was shocked to see the physical human wreckage of war: the burned, the crippled, the blinded, and the maddened victims of modern warfare. Additionally, Beckett, like almost the entire world, was shocked and stunned by the news-reels of the liberated concentration camps. The knowledge of and the very sight of the unspeakable horrors and the massive executions perpetrated from 1933 to 1945 on Jews and other people by the Germans, supposedly a civilized people, threw all thinking and feeling humans into a state of depression and despair. How could one believe again in a loving God? How could one ever consider that humans were better than animals or even as good? Human life surely was without meaning; it was absurd.

Beckett's existentialist dramas, beginning with *Waiting for Godot*, and many plays of the mid- to late twentieth century by other European and American dramatists, presented life as formless, purposeless, and futile. It was not bad enough that individual existence was experienced totally though the subjec-tive information provided by our limited senses; the dream of existence was in fact a nightmare. These modern plays came to be known as the Theater of the Absurd because they projected an irrational world and thus were so different from realistic drama. Today they are sometimes called postmodern.

Without Beckett's experiences during and after World War II and without the influence of existentialist philosophy, *Waiting for Godot* might never have been written. Indeed, Beckett, a novelist, might not have turned to the stage to provide a more immediate literary platform for his philosophical agenda.

SUGGESTED READINGS

Beckett, Samuel. *Waiting for Godot*. New York: Grove/Atlantic, 1976.

Ben-Zvi, Linda. *Samuel Beckett*. Boston: Twayne, 1986.

Knowlson, James. *Doomed to Fame: The Life of Samuel Beckett*. New York: Simon and Schuster, 1996.

6

John Osborne
Look Back in Anger
1956

John Osborne's play *Look Back in Anger* (1956) changed the direction of British drama. In the year it appeared, Arthur Miller hailed it as the only modern English play. British life was now under indictment. Osborne and many other new playwrights, including Harold Pinter, Arnold Wesker, John Arden, and Tom Stoppard, brought the young back into the theater with their radical departure from comfortable, complacent, but competent middle-class drawing-room drama that had dominated the mainstream British stage in the 1930s and into the 1950s. The revolution that Osborne fired up was political, but it was also a revolution in style. The new drama was raw as well as radical, and it freed the British theater from the shackles of improbable plots, happy endings, star turns, and, to an extent, conventional staging.

But the new British drama was more of a sociological phenomenon than a total artistic breakthrough. It seemed at the moment that the problem plays that had dominated British drama from Shaw's time on had been replaced by a drama of Beckettian ennui, without the abstraction of *Waiting for Godot*, for Osborne's characters in *Look Back in Anger*, like Beckett's, are defined not by their action but by their inaction. Nevertheless, the new plays had naturalistic settings, clear plots, and conventional characters. Later, British drama would reverse itself and take another radical turn when the 1950s negativism and Chekhovian inertia of *Look Back in Anger* would in the 1960s be replaced by the embracing of counterculture and antiwar activism.

BIOGRAPHICAL CONTEXT

John Osborne (1929–1994) was born in Fulham, London. His father was a commercial artist who died while Osborne was a child. His mother worked as a barmaid. In childhood, he was ill with rheumatic fever. At age 12, Osborne was sent to Belmont College, a minor private school in Devon, from which he was expelled for bad behavior. For the next 10 years, he worked at various jobs, including acting and stage managing in repertory theater. Osborne began to write plays in 1949, but he had no success until *Look Back in Anger* in 1956. From then on, he made his living as a writer.

In *The Entertainer* (1957), a success almost equal to *Look Back in Anger*, Osborne makes brilliant use of the music hall genre to record his disillusionment with post–World War II Britain. Osborne began his theatrical experimentation in *The Entertainer*, which he wrote for Lawrence Olivier, as he interspersed realistic scenes with music hall numbers in the Brechtian manner. Osborne used the decline of the music hall—and three generations of the Rice family—as symbols of the decline of Great Britain.

At that point in time, some critics considered Osborne to be the most important dramatist writing in English since Shaw. But his next play, *The World of Paul Slickey* (1959), a satirical protest musical insulting the establishment and critics, failed.

Luther (1961) was Osborne's third and final commercial success. In it, Osborne borrows from Brecht the idea of using a narrator to set time and place for each scene, and he used Martin Luther's own words to create a powerful character sketch of an Oedipal, troubled, and often ill person whose great intellect and integrity drove him on to rebel against the authority of a corrupt Church and change the history of the world.

Inadmissible Evidence (1964) is the story of Bill Maitland, a lecherous, alcoholic, pill-popping, wretched lawyer who gets by through profiting on the misery of others. He is the young and angry protagonist of *Look Back in Anger*, Jimmy Porter, in middle age, facing his spiritual bankruptcy.

A Patriot for Me (1965) is the true story of Alfred Redl, a Jewish officer in the Austro-Hungarian army at the turn of the twentieth century, who has risen from a working-class background and who needs to hide his homosexuality. Society drives Redl to suicide because he is totally an outsider: Jewish and gay. As one of the play's subjects is homosexuality, for five years the play was censored by the Lord Chamberlain, and it had to be performed in a club venue.

A Bond Honoured (1966) is about a clinical experiment in evil compounded with violence and blasphemy. The protagonist has raped his mother and lives incestuously with his sister, who also happens to be his daughter. In the social satire *Time Present* (1968), Pamela, an actress, and Constance, a member of Parliament, share a love. The play is unstructured and serves primarily as a platform for Osborne's liberal views on sexual relations. *Hotel in Amsterdam* (1968) is a play with little action on such subjects as love, friendship, fear of failure, and the nature of goodness.

West of Suez (1971) is a dark drama about a small group of English people living in a villa on a subtropical island. They represent a dying expatriate culture. In *A Sense of Detachment* (1973), Osborne breaks with almost all conventions of the theater, as interrupting "plants" in the audience provoke a battle between actors and spectators. In *Watch It Come Down* (1976), a commune of artists living in a converted railroad station manifest most sexual combinations.

From 1976 up to 1992, Osborne did not have a new play on the British stage. Osborne turned to television to earn a living. Finally, a sequel to *Look Back in Anger* was produced in 1992. In it, Jimmy Porter is now 36 years older, living comfortably in Shropshire, and vituperating against left-wing causes that he would have supported when he was a young man. Both Jimmy Porter and John Osborne had joined the philistines.

In 1970, Osborne received an honorary doctorate from the Royal College of Art in London. Osborne's life was not a happy one. He was married five times. He had one daughter.

PLOT DEVELOPMENT

Look Back in Anger is a play filled with black humor and despair. It is set in a shabby attic flat in a Midland town. The protagonist, the 25-year-old Jimmy Porter, comes from the working class. He has attended a provincial university that has prepared him for an establishment life, but he is contemptuous of that establishment because of class barriers kept in place by the bourgeoisie. Therefore, he makes money by selling candy in a market. Porter is angry because he believes that society is petty, mean, and hypocritical. He is disgusted with it, and he chooses to live outside it even though that decision may hurt his wife.

Porter is a revolutionary without any real cause. Frustrated, all he can do is hold his middle-class wife, Alison, hostage as a target for his frustration. But, of course, Porter's existence depends on the existence of that society he castigates. He tries to expose Alison to the realities of their lives in order to move her out of her state of complacency, but in that attempt the underlying anger that motivates his actions surges uncontrollably. Porter hopes Alison will fight back against his tirades, but it is not in her character to do so.

For many Britons dissatisfied with the so-called welfare state, especially the young, Jimmy Porter was the personification of their frustration and anger.

The cramped and sparsely furnished room that is the set cries out: social realism. Alison is a soft, attractive, attentive, but weak-willed wife. Also sharing the digs is their less educated friend, Cliff Lewis, whose bedroom is across the hall. Porter is an antihero whose continuous harangue both structures and informs the drama.

As act 1 opens, Jimmy and Cliff are sitting in easy chairs, reading the Sunday newspapers, while Alison, wearing one or her husband's old shirts, is working at the ironing board. Jimmy complains that the book review he is reading in the middle-class paper is half in French, and he asks Alison if that fact makes her feel ignorant. The implication is that it makes him feel ignorant. Alison, not wanting to fuel her husband's anger, replies that she wasn't listening. But Jimmy attacks her seemingly middle-class inertia, which irritates him.

Jimmy's next target is Cliff, whom he calls uneducated and ignorant. But Cliff won't be baited. Laid back and good-natured, Cliff agrees with his friend. Jimmy continues to vent his spleen at his helpless wife of three years. The room fills with unease.

From time to time, Jimmy and Cliff badger each other and engage in adolescent roughhousing that borders on homoerotic behavior, especially when it precedes or follows one of Jimmy's diatribes against women and "the entire flaming racket of the female." Ironically, it is the men in the scene who shout and scuffle or play a trumpet and the radio while the lone woman irons clothes.

Finally, in the childish play-battle, Jimmy pushes Cliff into the ironing board, and Alison is burned on the arm. Jimmy is sorry for a while, but Alison does not know how much longer she can stand living with her neurotic husband even though she is sure he loves her as she loves him.

The climax of the act takes place after Alison tries to inform Cliff that she is pregnant. Ironically, Jimmy is not willing to listen to Alison. Instead, he attacks her complacency, sexuality, and potential motherhood just when she is most vulnerable.

Act 2, scene 1, occurs in an evening two weeks later. Alison and her friend Helena, a young actress of Alison's social class, are preparing to go to church. Off in Cliff's room, Jimmy is playing jazz on his trumpet. Alison expresses her sorrow at being cut off from the kind of people she was brought up with and had always known before marriage to Jimmy. She is still unable to—and now fearful of—telling her husband of her pregnancy. When Jimmy and Cliff come in, Jimmy launches yet another vituperation against the English establishment. Jimmy always seems to need an audience for his tirades. His particular target this time is Alison's mother, and the virulent attack pains his wife.

Jimmy then reveals a source for his anger. He speaks of spending months watching his father die, and that feeling of helplessness made him the angry person he is. Helena begins to talk her friend into leaving her violent husband. After Jimmy is called out of the flat to take a phone call, Helena tells Alison that she has telegraphed Alison's father to come to the flat and take his daughter home. Jimmy returns to inform Alison that a close friend's wife has had a stroke and that he must go to London to be with her. He tells his wife that he needs her to go with him. Alison refuses, and Jimmy goes off by himself.

When act 2, scene 1, opens, Alison is packing to leave. Her father, Colonel Redfern, a kindly old soldier and clearly the kind of establishment figure whom Jimmy cannot stand, arrives to drive Alison home. When Jimmy returns to find Alison gone, he faces his enemy, Helena, in the flat, and he lashes out at her. But she is sexually excited by his fierceness, and the scene ends with Helena slapping Jimmy's face and then kissing him passionately.

Act 3, scene 1, takes place on an early Sunday evening several months later. The atmosphere in the flat is peaceful and relaxed. Jimmy and Cliff are reading the Sunday newspapers again, but it is Helena who is wearing Jimmy's old shirt, working at the ironing board. Jimmy begins a tirade on politics and against religion, but soon the three are singing. Like adolescents, Jimmy and Cliff again wrestle playfully until Cliff's shirt gets dirty. Helena takes it out to wash it, and Cliff informs Jimmy that he is going to move out of the flat and perhaps find a woman for himself. Helena returns with Cliff's shirt, and he takes it to the gas fire in his room so that it can dry out.

Jimmy and Helena are preparing to go out drinking, but the door opens, and Alison walks in. She says hello, and Jimmy says to Helena, "Friend of yours to see you," and leaves the room with the two women looking at each other as the curtain descends.

Act 3, scene 2, takes place a few minutes later. Alison tells Helena that she was mad to come to the apartment, but clearly she misses Jimmy terribly. She reports that she had a miscarriage, and the audience later learns that she will never be able to have a child again. The badly shaken Alison has no rancor for Helena. Her sorrow and helplessness moves Helena to the realization that she has done an evil thing. Meanwhile, Jimmy has been trying to dominate the scene by loudly playing his trumpet in the next room. Even though she too loves Jimmy, Helena chooses to depart rather than participate in a contest he would enjoy. As she leaves, she tells Alison that she would be a fool to go back to Jimmy. But Alison would rather crawl back and live with her angry husband than without him. For his part, Jimmy argues for understanding how difficult it has been to love and live with a woman who seemed to have everything in the world. He hoped that her love would allow for his faults. Now Alison is the sorry person.

Jimmy and Alison then revert to a childish world of role and game playing, replete with humiliations, that, nevertheless, allows them to be affectionate in a way they can't be in the real world. As the play concludes, Jimmy is being comforted by Alison, who has her arms around him. She has surrendered independence. She will be the mother substitute, servant, and bed partner he wants.

CHARACTER DEVELOPMENT

With the exception of the protagonist, the characters in this kitchen-sink drama (as opposed to drawing-room comedy) are distinguished by their ordinariness. Jimmy Porter (his name symbolizes working class) has the ability to use language as a sharp knife. He is a jazz-playing, ex–university student now earning a meager living in a candy stall. He is alternately sentimental, vicious, violent, self-pitying, and sadistic. In fact, egotistical self-pity has replaced commitment in his shaky marriage. Jimmy is not mature enough for marriage. He does not know how to live with and love a woman because he is consumed with anger. Simultaneously, he both needs women and fears them.

Nevertheless, Jimmy has some redeeming values. He is or has been loyal to some people, such as his dying father and his friend's mother who cared for him as if her were her own, who bought him the candy stall, and whom he cares enough about to travel to London to comfort her in the hospital.

Other characters are less complex than Jimmy. Alison, Jimmy's long-suffering wife, is an upper-middle-class young woman who has fallen in love unwisely. Her life has changed utterly, and she is unhappy as a household drudge. Oddly, she is unhappy because of change, while Jimmy is unhappy because nothing has changed for him.

Alison is kind, warm, well meaning, and maternal, which make her all the more vulnerable to her husband's exploitation. Tragically, she would have made an excellent mother, but that will never happen now. Alison is very much a woman of the 1950s. Despite her education, marriage seems to have been the major goal of her life. To today's young women, Alison seems pitiable.

Cliff, the sympathetic pal, tries to ameliorate the stresses in his friends' marriage. He cuddles up to Alison, and he horses around with Jimmy.

He seems not to have had a sexual relationship in his life, and until he suddenly matures in the play and flees the nest to find a woman to love, he is the surrogate child for his immature friends, unhappily playing house during the three years of their marriage.

The more Helena, Allison's predatory girlfriend, battles Jimmy, the more she becomes infatuated with him, and so her attempt to separate Alison from her husband, outwardly to help her friend, is really her way of getting Jimmy for herself. Ironically, she becomes his household drudge and the object of his misogynistic attacks.

The somewhat befuddled father, Colonel Redfern, represents upper-middle-class British people who were born in Edwardian times, spent their working lives in colonial administration, and found it almost impossible to understand the post–World War II Britain they returned to. Redfern is the most sympathetic and least complicated character in the drama. He does not hate Jimmy as his wife does. But he knew from the start that the marriage of Jimmy and Alison was going to be a rocky one to say the least. Nevertheless, he wished he had worked harder to understand his son-in-law.

THEMES

With the empire disintegrating, post–World War II Britain is a class battleground transformed in *Look Back in Anger* into a sadomasochistic war between the sexes. Bright but frustrated young working-class men, lacking educational and economic opportunities, took out their anger and hatred on women, preferably those of the middle class or upper middle class, who were the available establishment targets. Misogyny is Jimmy's main defensive weapon in his frustrated solitary war with the classes that hold all the power in society.

Young men like Jimmy Porter were still subject to military service. They resented having to give two years of their lives supporting the stifling status quo as they saw it. The main message of the play is that the frustration of angry young men like Osborne himself must be understood and reckoned with. The world wars and the continuing class war were not bringing an equalizing of opportunity. Like a storm-battered ship, Britain seemed to be drifting to destruction. Osborne implies that there never will be peace between the classes of society. He implies the possible breakup of British society by intimating that disappointed, disaffected, angry young men were powder kegs that would explode later.

Look Back in Anger is also a play about sexuality. Jimmy is a representative young man who is having a sexual crisis. He finds relating to women and understanding them extremely difficult. He was not close to his mother, so he substituted a friend's kind mother as an object of maternal love. He loves his wife but despises women in general even though he desperately needs them. In fact, he sees women as objects to be used. Only at the end of the play, when the reunited Alison and Jimmy revert to childhood and play a game of squirrel and bear, does the audience fully understand Jimmy's arrested maturity.

NARRATIVE STYLE

The language in *Look Back in Anger* adds to the impact of the drama. It is colloquial and full of taunts and put-downs as befitting a kitchen-sink drama. There is a raw naturalism in Jimmy Porter's diatribes. Clearly, Osborne opted for authenticity over poetry in contradiction to the poet-dramatist William Butler Yeats's famed advocacy for the sovereignty of words over physical representation. Jimmy and Alison are educated and can talk cleverly about literature, music, and sex, but they seem to do it more to impress the less educated Cliff, who tries to emulate it, than out of any deep concerns or convictions.

Osborne uses symbolism skillfully in *Look Back in Anger*. Alison represents the old establishment under attack and doomed to defeat by the angry proletariat. She accepts the defeat because it seems the only way she can help her husband find an identity that includes self-respect. But Alison is also giving up her identity and self-respect in a way that a post-1970s women's movement feminist would never do. In that respect, *Look Back in Anger* is a dated play, a true period piece.

The relationship between Jimmy and Cliff symbolizes male bonding with a slight homoerotic overtone. Cliff's leaving seems more of a loss for Jimmy than does Alison's departure.

Alison's father, the retired colonel of the British-officered Indian army, symbolizes the failures of the older generation—the empire builders—to pass on to the young generation a better nation with a coherent, workable, democratic social and economic plan. Victorious in wars, they nevertheless are exhausted. They are neither able to communicate with the young nor understand their pervasive ennui.

Look Back in Anger shows the detachment of the younger generation from the events of the time by their choice to live on society's sidelines. They participate in the life of the nation only by reacting to newspaper stories and verbally attacking distant targets like the intelligentsia, the clergy, and the "American Age." Osborne succeeded in awakening feeling in the British public for the plight of the alienated young who seemed hopeless and oddly burned out at so tender an age.

HISTORICAL CONTEXT

When World War II ended, Britain was victorious but exhausted. Millions of service personnel hoped that postwar Britain would be a more just and less class-ridden society with greater opportunity for higher education and advancement than before the war. The British public actually voted Winston Churchill and his Conservative Party out of office in 1945, but the new Labour Party government was able to do relatively little to effect social change. Despite the Education Act of 1944, opportunity for higher education was limited to a few. Oxford and Cambridge still dominated the educational system, and they and the so-called red-brick universities built in industrial cities in the nineteenth century could not accommodate the vast number of young people qualified for higher education. In 1946, as Britain struggled to rebuild from the war damage, the Cold War with the Soviet Union, an ally only a year before, commenced.

In the late 1940s, Britain had trouble with its colonies, especially India and Palestine, and the British government divided both and pulled out, leaving chaos in its wake. The British pound was radically devalued, and much of the rest of the British Empire was collapsing. In 1951, Churchill and the Conservatives returned to power, and even though young Queen Elizabeth succeeded to the throne in 1952, neither she nor Churchill could create educational and employment opportunities enough to satisfy the youth of Britain, some of whom turned to radical politics but most of whom experienced a loss of faith in their nation, feeling that the old politics and class system that so favored the privileged few would never change.

These events informed Osborne's view of his nation's dilemma, and he instilled that view into his malcontented antihero—Jimmy Porter.

SUGGESTED READINGS

Gilleman, Luc M. *John Osborne: Vituperative Artist: A Reading of His Life and Work.* New York: Routledge, 2002.
Hinchcliffe, Arnold P. *John Osborne*. Boston: Twayne, 1984.
Osborne, John. *Look Back in Anger*. New York: S.G. Phillips, 1957.

7

Harold Pinter
The Birthday Party
1958

Harold Pinter and Tom Stoppard have made contemporary British drama a significant part of world drama. Their plays are translated and performed around the globe. Both playwrights are indebted to the groundbreaking contribution to world drama that the Irish playwright and Nobel Prize–winning Samuel Beckett made in combining existential philosophy; an ontological vision of life as solitary, random, and absurd; and an antinaturalistic concept of dramaturgy, the prime example of which is *Waiting for Godot* (1953).

Pinter first saw *Waiting for Godot* in London in 1956, and he soon absorbed much of Beckett except that Pinter's plays are—on the surface at least—naturalistic. But both Pinter and Stoppard are influenced by Beckett in their trademark transmutation of banal language exchanges into sophisticated battles of wit surrounded by pregnant pauses. Pinter alone, however, combines the frightening with the farcical.

Pinter is also strongly influenced by the posthumously published novels of the Jewish Czech writer Franz Kafka (1883–1924), especially his novels *The Trial* (1925) and *The Castle* (1926), in which human beings are isolated and terrorized by unknown authorities. Like Kafka's characters, Pinter's characters experience loneliness, fear, terror, solitude, emptiness, despair, and the inability to communicate. They are often tormented by forces beyond their control regardless of their innocence or guilt. Pinter mocks reason. He has no faith in passion or the endurance of love. Value judgments, like good and evil, are either obscure, left to the audience, or totally banished. Thus, Pinter's plays have a purposeful ambiguity that allows for interpretation and even heated argument.

The Birthday Party has best been described as a comedy of menace. Like Beckett's *Waiting for Godot, The Birthday Party* was not understood at first, but when the critics finally caught on, the play entered the British modern repertory as a masterpiece. *The Birthday Party* is designed for any number of interpretations. Each audience member supplies his or her experiences to flesh out the meaning of the situation.

BIOGRAPHICAL CONTEXT

Harold Pinter was born in 1930 in impoverished East London. His father, Hyman, was a Jewish tailor, descended from Portuguese Jews named da Pinta. His mother was the former Frances Mann. An only child, Pinter grew up experiencing anti-Semitism and violence before and during World War II. When London was blitzed, Pinter was evacuated to the country with thousands of other children.

Pinter's education included local primary schools, the Hackney Downs Grammar School from 1943 to 1947, and the Royal Academy of Dramatic Art in 1948. When called for military service, Pinter declined as a conscientious objector, not wanting to be a part of the Cold War. He was fined for his decision.

In 1949, Pinter began his professional acting career, supplementing income with various nonacting jobs. In the early 1950s, he toured with the Anew McMaster's repertory company in Ireland and Donald Wolfit's classical repertory company in Britain. Pinter's career as a playwright began with the one-act play *The Room* (1956), set in a small, dilapidated flat from which the outside world seems menacing. *The Room* set the tone and coloration of much of Pinter's later work.

Pinter married the actress Vivien Merchant in 1956. They had a son and were divorced in 1980, when Pinter married the distinguished biographer Lady Antonia Fraser. Pinter has worked as a director of the National Theater. He has also made an important contribution to contemporary cinema by writing several outstanding screenplays. He has directed widely for the stage and acted in his own plays. Pinter's many honors include Commander, Order of the British Empire, awarded in 1966. The playwright has been a devoted activist for peace and human rights around the world.

The Dumb Waiter (1957), a one-act play, is a dark and menacing comedy about two hired gunmen waiting for the order to murder an unknown person. Pinter's first full-length drama is *The Birthday Party* (1958), in which visitors break down the protagonist and destroy his identity by playing on his fears while pretending to celebrate his birthday. *A Slight Ache* (1958) is about the psychological breakdown of a man named Edward after he has blinded and squashed a wasp. His eyes begin to ache as a match seller appears, a man who may have raped Edward's wife many years ago and who soon is seduced by her.

The Caretaker (1960) has two brothers struggling for power while a tramp is trying to ingratiate his way into their house and lives. *The Caretaker* is the drama that made the critics recognize that Pinter was a force in contemporary theater.

The Homecoming (1965), one of Pinter's commercial successes, focuses on a savage contest over a sexually desirable woman fought by a family of men. In *Old Times* (1971), a play about memory, a husband and wife battle over a girlfriend of the wife who may also once have been the husband's lover. The trio talk over old times, but what they say may or may not have happened. The wife and the girlfriend may or may not have been lesbian lovers. Although the girlfriend seems to hold the power, in the end it is the wife who is in control simply because she is less interested in winning.

No Man's Land (1974) has an impoverished poet who is trying to worm his way into the household of a celebrity colleague but who is thwarted by the watchful servants who orchestrate their employer's life and minister to his homosexual desires. Ultimately, the servants control both men's lives. *Betrayal* (1978) is a seemingly conventional love triangle until the audience realizes that the story is being played backward. It is one of Pinter's most popular and frequently performed dramas.

Family Voices (1981), originally written for radio, is an epistolary play with a mother's and a son's voices instead of written letters, although the monologues are referred to as letters. The story concerns a young man who has left his rural home to live in a large city. He has located a room in a rooming house run by an elderly woman who weans him from his affection for his mother because she wants a foster son. The play is a Freudian parable about coming to sexual maturity. *A Kind of Alaska* (1982) depicts a patient with sleeping sickness who is stressfully disoriented because of the new drug that revives him.

As the 1980s progressed, Pinter's plays became more politicized, as in *One for the Road* (1984), in which the protagonist's home is invaded by soldiers who arrest him, murder his son, rape his wife, torture him physically and mentally, and then are kind to him in order to bring him to conformity. *Mountain Language* (1988) is a powerful one-act play in which soldiers of a dictatorship use bureaucratic doublespeak to victimize women waiting outside a prison for news of their missing husbands. *Party Time* (1991) is reminiscent of *Mountain Language*. In this play, women, seemingly existing comfortably in society, worry about people lost in the past: a husband, a brother, and friends who have disappeared into the clutches of a totalitarian regime. The "disappeared" have left a great void in their lives.

In *Ashes to Ashes* (1996), Devlin questions a woman he is living with about her former lover, a factory owner. The woman, Rebecca, relates the story willingly despite the fact that the relationship was sadomasochistic. As the play progresses, Devlin becomes more abusive, but when Rebecca also reveals that her baby was taken away as she was about to board a train and that her former lover tore babies from screaming mothers, it becomes clear that Rebecca is a Holocaust survivor. Thus, obtaining sympathy, she gets the upper hand in her new relationship. Here Pinter, somewhat cryptically perhaps, finally confronts the Holocaust, an event and a theme he had touched on before but not explicitly addressed.

Celebration (2000) is a comic satire on the course, greedy, and ill-mannered nouveaux-riches. Pinter sees as a source of moral decay capitalism's materialism and stress on the individual's right selfishly to acquire whatever he or she can. The parvenus insulate themselves from the suffering in the world and are concerned only with power and sex. These later plays, cryptic and enigmatic, have received less attention from the public.

Pinter's drama depicts the human condition as full of unexpressed fears, often from unknown or unexpected sources, that must be battled but are seldom beaten. Survival is the best one can hope for. The likely outcome is Hobbesian: domination, exploitation, and victimization.

PLOT DEVELOPMENT

The Birthday Party is a play about the subjugation of its protagonist, Stanley Webber, a man in his late thirties who is living sedately and perhaps secretly in a somewhat seedy seaside boardinghouse. He is the only lodger. The proprietors Meg and Petey, a couple in their sixties, treat him as surrogate child. The family scene is decidedly dysfunctional as Stanley dominates Meg.

In act 1, during an ordinary breakfast complete with corn flakes and the morning newspaper, Meg announces that two strange men are coming to stay the night. This news makes Stanley apprehensive. The strangers, Goldberg and McCann, arrive and appear to be agents from an unknown person or organization. It is as if the intruders represent some repressive or fascist government—a familiar experience to many Europeans in the twentieth century. Indeed, the situation is surrealistically Kafkaesque. Meg announces that it is Stanley's birthday, although he vigorously denies it. But Meg is determined to give her surrogate son a party, and Goldberg demands it. Stanley seems to have met Goldberg before and is clearly upset.

Act 2 takes place in the evening. Stanley tries unsuccessfully to get Goldberg and McCann to leave the premises, but they refuse. When he tries to leave, Goldberg and McCann physically prevent him and then turn to badgering him. Stanley tries to get the upper hand over Goldberg by insulting him, but Goldberg is unmoved. A fight breaks out between the three men, but it is inconclusive, and Stanley remains trapped.

Petey, Meg, and Lulu, a local young woman, come in. Lulu attracts Goldberg. Drinks are poured, and the birthday party commences. Stanley is finally blindfolded and forced to play blindman's bluff. McCann, who has been holding Stanley's glasses, breaks them. The lights suddenly go off, and as the act ends, Goldberg and McCann converge on Stanley with menace.

Act 3 takes place the next morning. Meg wants to know when Stanley is coming down for breakfast. Petey is aware that something terrible has happened to Stanley, but he won't tell his wife, who goes shopping. Goldberg and McCann come down, and Petey tells them that he wants to get Stanley to a doctor. Goldberg won't let that happen. Petey leaves for a while, and Lulu enters. She is angry at Goldberg for the sexual liberties he took with her during the night, but Goldberg insists she enjoyed everything.

Lulu is menaced by McCann and Goldberg, and she leaves frightened. Stanley is brought in after a night of terror. He is clean shaven and no longer wearing the torn clothes of the night before. Instead, he is respectable, dressed in a suit. Stanley appears to have been brainwashed and is incapable of speaking or resisting his tormentors who verbally attack him again. When Petey returns, he tries to help Stanley, but Goldberg threatens him, and Petey backs off. As Stanley is led out to a waiting car, he looks and acts like a zombie, dressed to mock the society he has been fleeing from. In the end, Stanley's identity has been destroyed.

When Meg returns, Petey tells his wife nothing of what has transpired, and she remains blissfully ignorant of the fact that her surrogate son has been carted away.

Initially, Webber had struggled to hide his personal identity by being vague about his background and work. He has a right to his privacy and his individuality, but that is exactly what the Orwellian state does not want him or us to maintain.

The audience always wonders who Stanley is, beyond formerly working as a pianist as is mentioned. What has he done? Just who are his abductors? Are they government agents, terrorists, or criminals? Where do the three men go as the play ends? Will Stanley die on his nonbirthday? Is torture or prison his fate? Pinter leaves it to the audience to contemplate the possible terror a knock on the door can bring to anyone in the modern world.

CHARACTER DEVELOPMENT

Stanley Webber is the central character in *The Birthday Party*. He is a complicated, mysterious character, part bully and part coward. He is rational at first and then grows irrational. Stanley has a secret in his past that the audience never learns. He seems to be on the run, hiding in the run-down boardinghouse that has no other guests than himself until the ominous arrival of Goldberg and McCann. The audience does not see in what way he was tortured in his bedroom overnight. Only the results are apparent, for Stanley has been turned into a helpless, childlike idiot.

Goldberg is the most articulate character in *The Birthday Party*. He controls McCann and all the people in the house. He dominates them with his long monologues that seem designed to show that tyranny is deeply rooted in ordinary behavior as well as self-absorption. Goldberg is Jewish and thus an outsider to British society, even though his upbringing appears to have been replete with middle-class English values. But the audience can never be sure of the truth of his statements. For example, he keeps changing his first name.

McCann is Irish and thus an outsider too. Interestingly, he is called by different first names by Goldberg. McCann is Goldberg's sidekick, and unlike his boss, he has reservations about what they are doing to Stanley. It appears that it may be his task eventually to kill him. Audiences who know Sean O'Casey's *Juno and the Paycock* may see Goldberg and McCann partly as buddies like Boyle and Joxer but also like the two "die-hard" assassins who come to take the pitiful and broken Johnny to his execution. It is quite possible to see McCann and Goldberg as avengers capturing a traitor to the Irish Republican Army, a terrorist organization that battles British rule in Northern Ireland.

Meg is sweet, sympathetic, motherly, and not very bright. Unlike her husband Petey, she is unaware of what is happening to Stanley. She is a woman without power in her home and in her subservient role of cooking and nurturing.

Petey is the kind of person who is reluctant to get involved. He tolerates Stanley and is accepting of his wife without showing affection, but he is more interested in his job as a beach chair attendant, his chess game, and the morning newspaper than he is in what terrible things are happening in his home. When he has seen Stanley upstairs for a moment and realizes that his surrogate son has been hurt, he wants to take Stanley to a doctor, but when Goldberg insists that he will do that, Petey defers to the more powerful man. When Petey finally tries to help Stanley and Goldberg threatens to take him along with Stanley in the big car waiting, he backs away out of fear.

Lulu, a bimbo living in the neighborhood, sleeps with Goldberg and awakens to regret whatever selfish things he did to her. She too is a victim of Goldberg.

THEMES

The major theme in *The Birthday Party* is the vulnerability of all people to terrorism. It is a theme out of Kafka. Brutal men are always available to do horrible things to other human beings in the name of a cause, a country, or organized crime. There is nothing one can do to protect oneself from arbitrary selection for punishment. Furthermore, one's neighbors and friends will not help you when the agents of evil come knocking because the possible cost to them is more than they are willing to pay. That cost is that they also could then be caught up in a dragnet of cruelty. Pinter is warning us.

Pinter chooses to assault his audience with his understated pictures of brutality. Torture is perhaps more terrible when one imagines what may be happening behind a closed door. Another theme in *The Birthday Party* is the total lack of any humane values in society that could mitigate controlling entities like a fascist state or a terrorist organization as their diabolic minions make their appointed rounds.

In the end, Stanley and any other arbitrary victim stands alone and vulnerable in an existential loneliness waiting for whatever will happen.

NARRATIVE STYLE

Conventionally, plot in drama provides certain actions that bring a play to life. It folds character and idea into dialogue and progressive movement. In Pinter, plot slowly reveals an emotional state. Dramatic situation often replaces traditional causation. That concept is exciting in its freshness but also limiting in its lack of the rising and falling that proceeds from unfolding revelations through the alternation of suspense and surprise.

Pinter is a master of creating mood. In *The Birthday Party*, he turns the banalities, repetitiousness, and emptiness of life into elements of anxiety as Stanley and the audience confront the unknown. Pinter intersperses comedy with tension by employing humorous children's games, riddles, one-liner jokes, rapid patter, and cross-talk routines. The scenes of interrogation in the play are masterful examples of using language as an instrument of torture as Goldberg and McCann bombard Stanley with shards of sentences and chains of interlocking utterances so that their victim seems to be bound by language.

HISTORICAL CONTEXT

Harold Pinter was born into the Great Depression. He saw the meanness of soul-destroying poverty in London's tenement-filled East End. That experience as much as anything intellectual made Pinter a passionate socialist. In his youth, sharing the ignorance of tens of millions of people about the truth of life in the Soviet Union and the cruelty of Stalin, he saw communism as a way to ameliorate the economic disparities in society.

As the Nazis grew more menacing in Germany in the late 1930s, Pinter in England was close enough to witness the virulent, almost insane anti-Semitism that the German people—a supposedly civilized people—embraced. Fascism was the great enemy of humankind. In the late 1930s, it seemed to be flowing even into Great Britain, and after the Germans began World War II by invading Poland in September 1939, the Jews of Britain feared that the enemy would cross the English Channel and treat them as they did the Jews of Germany, Holland, Belgium, and soon France. Jews would be registered, segregated, robbed, deported to concentration camps, and murdered. The source of some of Pinter's nightmarish scenes surely are his childhood fears of becoming yet another Jewish child seized by the Gestapo and taken to a concentration camp to be gassed and cremated.

The Cold War—1946 to 1991—was a highly polarized and politicized period in modern history. Pinter, like so many artists and writers, found new terrors in the arms race, nuclear weapons, Soviet gulags, and neocolonial wars like the Soviet invasion of Hungary in 1956 and the American involvement in Vietnam from 1964 to 1972. The artists and writers became activists in the causes of safety and justice for all humankind. Even in his seventies, Pinter is ready to join peace activists demonstrating against war and injustice.

SUGGESTED READINGS

Billington, Michael. *The Life and Work of Harold Pinter*. London: Faber and Faber, 1996.

Pinter, Harold. *The Birthday Party*. New York: Grove/Atlantic, 1989.

Pinter, Harold. *The Room*. New York: Grove/Atlantic, 1989.

8

Tom Stoppard
Rosencrantz and Guildenstern Are Dead
1966

Tom Stoppard, like Harold Pinter, followed the lead of Samuel Beckett in incorporating existentialist philosophy, relativism, and the Theater of the Absurd into his plays. Like Pinter, Stoppard is internationally recognized as one in Britain's long line of distinguished dramatists who have been thinkers and who continue the Theater of Ideas introduced by Shaw at the end of the nineteenth century. Like Shaw, Stoppard is a brilliant master of intellectual comedy. He is a dazzler who fires off bursts of sparkling comedic wordplay and who blends complicated plots with profound themes so that he has moved modern British drama in the direction of exhilarating cerebral aerobics. Stoppard is also a humanist committed to philosophical and scientific inquiry. He probes the limitations of individual existence, the power of the life force, and the ephemeral nature of love.

Stoppard's first full-length play, *Rosencrantz and Guildenstern Are Dead* (1966), in which two minor characters in Shakespeare's *Hamlet* witness the unfolding tragedy and then are swept up in it, brought Stoppard instant recognition as a significant playwright in the Shavian and Beckettian traditions.

BIOGRAPHICAL CONTEXT

Tom Stoppard (b. 1937) came into the world as Tomás Straüssler in Zin, Czechoslovakia (now the Czech Republic), the second son and last child of Eugen and Martha Becková Straüssler. Eugen, a company physician for the Bata shoe manufacturing company, was an assimilated Jew. Martha had both Gentile and Jewish grandparents. These facts were critical because Germany was preparing war on Europe and Hitler's virulent anti-Semitism was well known. But Stoppard did not learn he was Jewish until years later. In 1939, as the German invasion of Czechoslovakia was imminent, the family, helped by the benevolent company, fled to the British colony of Singapore. When the Japanese attacked Singapore in 1942, the British evacuated Mrs. Straüssler and the boys to Darjeeling, India. Eugen fatally chose to remain behind until the last possible minute, as he was badly needed for the tending of the wounded in the hospital. When he finally left, his unarmed ship was sunk by the Japanese, and presumably he drowned.

In November 1945, in Calcutta, Martha married Major Kenneth Stoppard of the British army, attached to the Indian army. Kenneth was a conservative Briton who was proud to have made his Jewish stepsons British boys. The family arrived in England and eventually settled in Bristol in 1946. As a schoolboy in England, Tomás became Tommy Stoppard, and his brother Petr became Peter. In fact, they had replaced the Czech language with English even before they left India.

Stoppard was educated at the Dolphin School, Nottinghamshire, from 1946 to 1948, and then he attended Pocklington School, Yorkshire, from 1948 to 1954. Next, Stoppard went to work as a journalist with the *Western Daily Press* in Bristol. Four years later, he joined the Bristol *Evening World*. While working at the *Evening World*, Stoppard became interested in the theater, and he moved to London to review drama for *Scene*, a short-lived magazine.

After publishing three short stories and writing two radio plays and a television script, Stoppard received a 1964 Ford Foundation grant to attend a colloquium in Berlin for promising young playwrights. For the occasion, he wrote a short Shakespearean send-up called *Rosencrantz and Guildenstern Meet King Lear*. That became *Rosencrantz and Guildenstern Are Dead*, produced at the Edinburgh Festival in 1966 and the National Theatre at the Old Vic in 1967. Stoppard's playwriting career was well under way. His rise to prominence in the theater was meteoric. In 1978, Stoppard was made Commander, Order of the British Empire. He was knighted in 1997 and elevated to the Order of Merit by Queen Elizabeth II in 2000.

Of Stoppard's many successful screen and television plays, the most famous is the movie *Shakespeare in Love*. Of course, the hero is a playwright.

Stoppard married Jose Ingle in 1965. They had two sons. The marriage was dissolved in 1971. He married Miriam Moore-Robinson (born Miriam Stern) in 1972. The couple had two children. They were divorced in 1992. Stoppard had a long-term relationship with the actress Felicity Kendall until 1998.

In *Rosencrantz and Guildenstern Are Dead* (1966), Stoppard foregrounds two little people, university friends of Prince Hamlet, who have been summoned by

King Claudius and Queen Gertrude to Elsinor to spy on their friend. They are nonheroic protagonists who at last have their play, although, like the rest of us, they mostly wait and watch in the wings of history.

Jumpers (1968), an intellectual farce and murder mystery, has a team of philosophical gymnasts on stage "illustrating" the tortuous discourses of George Moore, a real-life moral philosopher preparing to compete with Duncan McFee, a logical positivist, for a chair in logic, while his wife, Dotty, has an affair with Sir Archbold Jumpers, the head of the philosophy department, who also manages the "Jumpers."

In *Travesties* (1974), Stoppard theorizes about the relationship between politics and art. He has Lenin, James Joyce, and the Dadaist artist Tristan Tzara, living in Zürich at the same time, while a British official, Henry Carr, does not see the significance of this juxtaposition. The revolutionary artist and the revolutionary politician share the same ambition: changing the world.

Every Good Boy Deserves Favour (1977) deals with injustice as seen through a child's eyes. *Night and Day* (1978) signifies journalistic freedom as a way of creating positive political change.

The Real Thing (1982), more naturalistic than most of his plays, is Stoppard's innovative adventure in writing a traditional marital and sexual farce. *Hapgood* (1988) is the name of a British female spy who works with a German, trying to find out if secrets have leaked to the Soviets. In Stoppard, secret agents may be double or triple. Stoppard wonders what is illusion and what is reality in the world of spies. *Arcadia* (1993) combines chaos theory and the laws of thermodynamics with English landscape gardening of the early nineteenth century. The significance of the latter is because that was the time when the history of ideas was shifting from neoclassicism to romanticism.

India Ink (1995) is partly a detective story and partly a love story. The comedy hinges on the farcical misinterpretation of the past by academics, as Stoppard focuses on the aesthetic drawbacks of imperial influence. *The Invention of Love* (1997) is about the repressed gay poet A. E. Housman, in his old age, remembering his youthful, unconsummated love for an athletic classmate at Oxford. The title is ironic, for love cannot be invented, although the poet tries to do that.

The Coast of Utopia (2001) is a trilogy of plays requiring nine hours for performance. In them, Stoppard brilliantly explores the satisfactions, excitement, and the pitfalls of the life of the mind. The trilogy focuses on a group of mid-nineteenth-century Russian intellectuals for whom the term "intelligentsia" was coined. The goal of *The Coast of Utopia* is to identify an alternative opposition to communism that through humanistic gradualism could have succeeded where communism so catastrophically failed. The first play,

Voyage, is set in 1833 on a country estate where a young radical, Mikhail Bakunin, falls prey to the seduction of revolution. In *Shipwreck,* Bakunin sees that his dreams and his efforts are not without evil results. In *Salvage,* the hero comes to a Tolstoyan conclusion: one must focus on the immediate work and not the distant end, which may be a trap because the world will always be imperfect.

PLOT DEVELOPMENT

In *Rosencrantz and Guildenstern,* we catch only glimpses of the main-stage tragedy: *Hamlet.* The young men are almost indistinguishable from each other and have little free will. They are the pawns of the mighty who have almost no feeling or concern for the lowly. Required to inform on and betray their friend Prince Hamlet, Rosencrantz and Guildenstern are very poor spies. They try to manipulate the prince, but he easily outfoxes them.

Stoppard has deconstructed *Hamlet.* He has given us a vastly different "reading" of Shakespeare's play, one that says that chance, not fate, is the determinant in the human experience. Rosencrantz and Guildenstern are executed off stage in Stoppard's play as in Shakespeare's, but at the end of Stoppard's play our sympathies are with our peers, the poor students, and not with the royals and their courtiers.

The drama opens with Rosencrantz alone on the stage. He is soon joined by Guildenstern. They are on their way to Elsinor, the Danish capital, at the request of the new king, Claudius. They are amusing themselves by tossing coins, and Guildenstern is perplexed that heads turns up 85 times in a row. The seeming violation of the law of probability is foreboding to Guildenstern but not to the more optimistic Rosencrantz.

Soon they are joined by a troop of traveling players much down on their luck. Both parties will turn up in the palace of Elsinor, where the students are instructed by Claudius and Queen Gertrude to find out why their school friend Hamlet seems to be mad. Sadly, the students are not perspicacious enough to see in the players' rehearsal of the melodramatic tragedy *The Murder of Gonzogo* the foretelling of their own betrayal by their royal "friend" and their execution.

Act 2 begins with the students encountering their friend Hamlet. They are not successful in getting Hamlet to explain his strange behavior, for he is clearly more clever than they are. They also fail Claudius when he orders them to find the body of Polonius, whom Hamlet has accidentally killed. Finally, Claudius sends them as an escort for Hamlet, whom he has banished to England. There Claudius plans, by means of a letter entrusted to the bunglers, to have the English king kill the troublesome Danish prince.

Act 3 takes place on the ship bound for England. Hamlet, so much sharper than his blundering schoolmates, steals the royal letter, reads it, and replaces it with one ordering their deaths. The prince never understands the dilemma his poor friends are in: caught between loyalty to a friend and a royal command. The young men are simply of no significance to him.

After pirates attack the ship and Hamlet escapes, Rosencrantz and Guildenstern open the letter and learn of their forthcoming doom. Resigned to their fate, they wonder if there was a time in the beginning of their story in which they could have said no. If so, they missed it and the chance to change their fate. Stoppard's play ends with the scene in Shakespeare's in which two ambassadors from England, having come with news from their king, only to find Claudius, Gertrude, Laertes, and Hamlet dead, announce to Horatio, the truly loyal friend, that "Rosencrantz and Guildenstern are dead." In death, the commoners have joined the aristocrats; the standers-by have joined the principals in the catastrophe.

CHARACTER DEVELOPMENT

As in Shakespeare's *Hamlet,* Rosencrantz and Guildenstern are hardly distinguishable from each other. They are young men who are inadequate for the task that chance and the playwright have set out for them. They must spy, but they are unequipped for spying. They simply are not duplicitous by nature. In their very blundering, incompetent ordinariness, they ultimately find self-recognition and evoke pity in the audience. Rosencrantz and Guildenstern learn nothing from their participation in a tragedy except that they have had no control over the parts they play in the events leading to their execution. Their struggle is so far from monumental that they appear almost antlike in the world of kings and princes—and even performing artists.

The Player King, the leader of the acting troupe of tragedians, is someone always willing to perform whatever a paying audience desires. In his pliability, he is always able to one-up Rosencrantz and Guildenstern, who are able to be only their singular selves. When, on the road to Elsinor, the Player King latches on to the credulous youths, he and his protean troupe become the symbol of the immortality of an art that is as much about dying and death as any. Rosencrantz and Guildenstern are soon to die. The actors die many times on the stage. They make spectacle of dying, but they do not, of course, die in the flesh. The Player King says, "We're *actors*—we're the opposite of people."

THEMES

In *Rosencrantz and Guildenstern Are Dead,* Stoppard implies that we human beings are minor characters in a drama of our time, one that is beyond our comprehension. We are dependent on recognition by higher-ups who themselves cannot control their fate. Indeed, neither fate nor free will exist. Despite our frenzied activities, our outcome is a matter of chance and accident. The depressing relativity of our existence is terrifying. As the coin-tossing scene at the opening of the drama implies, life itself is a game of chance.

Rosencrantz and Guildenstern is a drama about death. Only the players are good at dying, but then, when they "die," they are not really dying. If they were actually dying, they would be no better at it than we are. All Rosencrantz and Guildenstern know at the final curtain is that the only beginning is birth and the only end is death.

In *Rosencrantz and Guildenstern,* Stoppard embraces existentialism, the philosophy that informed all of Beckett's plays and in which despairing individuals in a Godless universe are perceived as having little or no control of their destiny. Although they have a little free will in minor matters, people are carried along in the aimless, raging river of life to an unknown. Almost all human beings are like Rosencrantz and Guildenstern, or Vladimir and Estragon, in that we see into the glass of life very darkly indeed. A few figures—a prince or a president, for example—experience tragedy. The rest of their contemporaries endure the catastrophes their masters create.

NARRATIVE STYLE

Particularly clever in *Rosencrantz and Guildenstern* is Stoppard's sketchy presentation of Shakespeare's play by having Shakespeare's characters speak a few of their lines and by having Rosencrantz and Guildenstern observe pieces of either wordless or unheard action on the part of the original characters in the manner of the dumb shows of the itinerant players. The effect is to distance the protagonists from the action like people observing some great political figures in conversation but standing too far away to hear their words.

In homage to Beckett, Stoppard employs stychomythia: alternating one-line speeches to produce a hypnotic, poetic effect similar to the pattern used by Vladimir and Estragon in *Waiting for Godot.*

Rosencrantz and Guildenstern is a high comedy of ideas, spiced with elements and moments of farce. It is a particularly difficult kind of play to write because of the possibility of wearing out the audience with conundrums, firing ideas over their heads, or having many lose sight of the argument. Stoppard's great achievement in *Rosencrantz and Guildenstern Are Dead* is that argument and action are perfectly entwined.

HISTORICAL CONTEXT

Although Pinter and Stoppard were born in the same fateful decade, the 1930s—Pinter at the beginning and Stoppard toward the end—they reacted differently to World War II and the Cold War. Whereas Pinter fully absorbed the terror of fascism and the horror of the Holocaust and thus became a social and political activist, Stoppard, sheltered from anti-Semitism by being absorbed into the mainstream of British life, reacted to the current events of his time by choosing to be a nonpolitical artist. Stoppard rose and dwells intellectually and artistically above the fray. His realm is that of philosophy. His path to artistic truth is through intellectual discourse with which he presents to his audience the pathos, absurdity, relativity, and grim humor of life. Thus, he illustrates the uncertainties of the world.

SUGGESTED READINGS

Billington, Michael. *Stoppard the Playwright*. London: Methuen, 1987.

Nadel, Ira. *Tom Stoppard: A Life*. New York: Palgrave Macmillan, 2002.

Rusinko, Susan. *Tom Stoppard*. Boston: Twayne. 1986.

Stoppard, Tom. *Rosencrantz and Guildenstern Are Dead*. New York: Grove/Atlantic, 1976.

9

Brian Friel
Translations
1980

Brian Friel is Ireland's greatest living playwright. His dramas are renowned the world over. For many Irish people, including hyphenated Irish living in many countries, Friel speaks for Ireland. In some ways, he is uniquely qualified to do so. He is a Roman Catholic born in the Protestant-dominated British province of Northern Ireland. He was educated in the North and in the Republic. He has eschewed living in Dublin, the Irish capital, and instead resides in the distant rural County Donegal of the Republic, close to the border with County Londonderry in British Ulster. County Donegal was historically part of Ulster until the partition of Ireland after the approval of the Anglo-Irish peace treaty by the Dáil (Irish Parliament) in 1922. Thus, Friel lives and works on both sides of a contested border divided by religion, culture, nationalism, and to some extent even language, as Irish is taught in the schools of the South but not in those of the North.

Translations is by consensus Friel's masterpiece. Although set in the 1830s in the north of Ireland, it reflects the contemporary political situation in which it was written (late 1970s) and that largely still exists in the early years of the twenty-first century: potential and kinetic conflict along a religious and cultural fault line.

BIOGRAPHICAL CONTEXT

Brian Friel (b. 1929) was born near Omagh, County Tyrone, where his father taught school. In 1939, when Friel was 10, the family moved to the city of Derry (Londonderry to Protestants in Northern Ireland), and he received his early education at the Long Tower School, the school in which his father taught. He continued his study at St. Columb's College there. Friel spent two years at the Catholic seminary at Maynooth College, without receiving ordination, and in 1948 he enrolled in Belfast's St. Joseph's Teacher Training College, after which he was a schoolmaster in primary and intermediary schools in Derry from 1950 to 1960. In that year, his first play, *The Francophile*, was staged at the Ulster Group Theatre in Belfast. It was later adapted for radio as *A Doubtful Paradise*. His second and third plays, *The Enemy Within* (1962), a history play set in the sixth century on St. Columba's Iona, and *The Blind Mice* (1963), a problem play about loyalties within and without the Church, are, like *The Francophile*, little regarded today.

Writing after work during his teaching career, Friel had much success as a short-story writer for the *New Yorker* and other magazines. Meanwhile, the BBC produced his radio plays. Friel's short-story collections include *The Saucer of Larks* (1962), *The Gold in the Sea* (1966), and *Selected Stories* (1979), republished as *The Diviner* (1982). The skillfully crafted stories are about Ireland's North. They sing the nostalgic song of rural loss, and they mark the transient but precious moments of life as Friel's characters seek a meaning beyond survival.

Marriage to Anne Morrison came in 1954 while Friel was still teaching. The couple has five children. In 1963, Friel traveled to America to observe, work with, and learn from the distinguished Irish director Tyrone Guthrie in what eventually became the Tyrone Guthrie Theater of Minneapolis. There, Friel acquired the technique of skillfully building plays as he understudied Guthrie in the ways of the professional theater.

The great historical, political, and social event of Friel's life was the eruption of "The Troubles," the civil war in Ulster between nationalists who wished union with the Republic and Loyalists who wished the North to remain in the United Kingdom. It began in 1968 in Derry with Catholic demonstrations for civil rights. Over the next four years, there were marches and countermarches, the breakdown of law and order, and the massacre of 14 Catholic marchers by British soldiers. With continuing terrorism, reprisals, assassinations, and bombings, Northern Ireland disintegrated into a fearful world of police and soldiers facing off against guerrillas, with a civilian population held hostage to a vast international failure of political imagination. In that maelstrom, Friel's art was politicized, if only for the time being.

A significant result of that politicizing was the founding of the Field Day Theatre Company in 1980 by Friel and Stephen Rea in Derry with the Guildhall as its venue. Its raison d'être was the production of plays that would radicalize audiences, reinvigorate the political consciousness in Irish arts, and perhaps bring peaceful political and social change to Northern Ireland and reconciliation to the island. Field Day was an institutional phenomenon that was not restricted entirely to theater. With Derry as its epicenter, it embraced several cultural facets, including publishing. The Northern Ireland poet Seamus Heaney (later to win the Nobel Prize for Literature), the critic Seamus Deane, and the actor Stephen Rea were among the Irish luminaries associated with Field Day early on.

Translations (1980), the story of a small, remote, early nineteenth-century community about to change irrevocably, was the new northern company's first and greatest production. It should be noted that Friel has not been exclusively associated with one company. His plays have premiered in the Abbey more than elsewhere, but they have also opened at Dublin's Gaiety, Olympia, and Gate Theatres; the Helen Hayes Theater and the Longacre Theater in New York; and the Royal Court Theatre and the National Theatre in London.

Besides *Translations*, major plays of Brian Friel are *Philadelphia, Here I Come!* (1967), about the private and public personae of a young man about to emigrate, which established his national and international reputation; *The Loves of Cass McGuire* (1966), about the returning of an exile (an old derelict, drunken, embarrassing, unwanted Irish American woman); and *The Lovers* (1967), which includes two plots: "Winners," in which two school dropouts, one of them a girl, dream of their future although they will die in a boating accident; and "Losers," a comedy in which a middle-age bachelor tries to prevent the mother of the spinster he is wooing from learning of his intentions. *Crystal and Fox* (1968) shows how Fox Melarkey, the head of a rundown traveling show, destroys his family, his business, his identity, his life, and his wife's life in his vain attempt to recapture an ideal and innocent world. *The Mundy Scheme* (1969) has Friel satirically wondering if the Republic is actually a nation or a pastoral playground for Europeans and Americans.

The Freedom of the City (1973) is Friel's angry reaction to the shooting of Irish protestors by the British army in 1972, and *Volunteers* (1975), like its predecessor, is based on contemporary events, this time in Dublin, where the city council is destroying the Viking archaeological site in order to build office buildings and some political prisoners volunteer to work to save what bits of history can be saved while their fellow prisoners brand them traitors and threaten their lives.

Aristocrats (1979) is an elegy to the end of the Irish country mansion, better known as the "Big House," as well as an anatomy of a declining Catholic family. *Faith Healer* (1979) is about waiting for a creative miracle and the dire results when it seems to happen. *Translations* (1980) laments both the near death of the Irish language and the decline of the Irish village. In contrast, *The Communication Cord* (1982) finds Friel unsentimentalizing Irish rural life. *Making History* (1988) deals with the way the future chooses to remember the trials and tribulations of the great Irish soldier Hugh O'Neill and the historically pivotal battle of Kinsale in 1601.

Even more popular than *Translations*, *Dancing at Lughnasa* (1990) is a ritual drama where the ancient pagan Irish festival of music and dance, the Lughnasa, is reflected in the lives of five unmarried sisters and the unreliable and unstable men in their lives. *Wonderful Tennessee* (1993) is like a medieval text in which each speaker tells her or his personal story, which may or may not be fully truthful. In *Molly Sweeney* (1994), Friel, like John Millington Synge in *The Well of the Saints*, examines blindness from the viewpoint of a woman born in it who must suddenly consider the possibility of partial vision and how that would change and complicate her life. *Give Me Your Answer, Do!* (1997) is a despairing parable of a novelist's inability to handle the emotional demands on him made by wife, mentally handicapped child, relatives, and friends when his own creativity has dried up and financial ruin is imminent.

For the most part, it is County Donegal and Derry City that make up the environment and inspiration for Friel's plays. It is an economically depressed region of high unemployment and much emigration, with an artificial dividing line running through it, the boundary between the Republic and the British province of Northern Ireland, where on the Northern Ireland side Roman Catholics have endured discrimination and political repression at least since 1922 while sectarian strife has simmered and boiled ever since 1969.

In 1987, the Republic of Ireland gave Friel the highest recognition it has for an artist: he was appointed to the Irish Senate.

PLOT DEVELOPMENT

Translations is considered one of the most important Irish political plays ever written. It criticizes the ultimate colonization of Ireland in the early nineteenth century, brought about by the surveyors of the British Army Corps of Engineers who mapped and renamed the countryside in order to facilitate military movement and control. The mapmakers and surveyors may have been well meaning in themselves, but they participated in the devastation of an ancient culture, facilitating its replacement by a colonial culture. In the drama, English is at war with Irish Gaelic and is winning. The struggle is symbolized by its effect on a single family, the O'Donnells, in Baile Beag, the small town's old name, or Ballybeg, its new colonial appellation.

The play is set in Baile Beag's hedge school barn. The school is teaching Greek, Latin, and elementary subjects in Irish, the language under attack. The hedge schools, including Baile Beag's, are about to be superseded by the National Schools with all instruction in English. The schoolmaster is Hugh, a heavy-drinking pedagogue in his sixties who stands for the fading authority of the Celtic past. Hugh expects to become a headmaster of one of the new National Schools, but he will be denied the post to a large extent because of his drinking. Manus, his older son, also a teacher, is lame from childhood because of the carelessness of his drunken father. Manus loves Maire, a beautiful student, and expects to marry her.

Hugh's younger son is Owen, who has been prospering in Dublin but who has just returned to Baile Beag with the British Army Corps of Engineers to serve as a translator for the men mapping and renaming the north. Owen, who has integrated into the greater world of the British Empire, is uneasy with his mission because he still retains feelings for his Irish culture and community. He altruistically hopes to be an instrument of conciliation between the culture of his family and that of the colonial establishment.

Owen's friend, the sensitive English lieutenant Yolland, falls in love with Maire, and she falls in love with him. Although he speaks no Irish and she no English, they soon find that love has a powerful language of its own. It needs no translation. Their tragic love affair, akin to that of Shakespeare's young lovers—Romeo and Juliet—is the central event in *Translations* and the turning point of the play. The audience is led to hope against hope that their love, Yolland's idealizing of the beauty of the landscape, and the warmth of the Irish way of life will serve as the first cable in a great bridge linking the two cultures, but *Translations* is a tragedy, and, as history proves, the bridge is never to be completed because Manus becomes jealous after he is informed by Sarah—a formerly mute young woman whom he has barely managed to teach to speak a little—that Yolland and Maire have embraced.

Yolland suddenly disappears. No one seems to know what has happened to him, but Sarah, who cares for Manus, has informed the Donnelly twins: violent young men from the part of the community most against the British. The British commander, Captain Lancey, assumes that his lieutenant has been captured by the Irish, and he brutally orders that if Yolland is not returned immediately, all the livestock of the people will be killed, the houses torn down, and the inhabitants driven from the area. Manus, heartbroken and sensing a tragedy unfolding, flees Baile Beag, and presumably he will be hunted down as a prime suspect in the disappearance. Presumably also, Yolland has been murdered. Owen, the mediator, the translator, the would-be bestrider of cultures, has failed and does not know what now to do with his life. But he must choose between his culture and his sure knowledge that Ireland's future and his own best interest lie with the colonial power. With his native town in flames and his dreams wrecked, he chooses Ireland and leaves to join the Donnellys in what must be a futile revolt.

Maire, stunned and heartbroken by the disappearance of Yolland, asks Hugh to teach her English in case her lover should return but also with the possibility that she will emigrate to England or America to escape the memory of her loss and the madness of her time.

In the end, the militant Donnelly twins are in charge of the people, the revengeful occupiers are savaging the land, Yolland is dead, and two obsolete old men, Hugh and his oldest student, Jimmy Jack, are getting drunk and are mourning the burning of ancient Carthage while their own town is ablaze.

Translations is a play of mistakes. Yolland and Maire, naively following their hearts, cross a contested frontier: exogamy, or attempting to mate across a line of racial or political enmity. Owen and Yolland make mistakes in translations. Yolland even thinks his friend's name is Roland. Good-hearted Owen believes he can bring his employers and his people together with mutual respect and understanding, but he is mistaken because he has not realized the power language has over a culture. Captain Lancey, possessor of military power and oblivious to its limitations, has overreacted in punishing an entire community for the possible criminal act of a very few, thus ensuring anger, resistance, hatred, and continual guerrilla warfare against his mapping enterprise. And poor Manus, his heart broken, his town destroyed, unwisely limps off with nowhere to go and sure to be captured on suspicion that he was involved in Yolland's disappearance.

Finally, although communication through language, human understanding, love, and compassion have broken down and failed tragically, *Translations* succeeds brilliantly because the play proves the efficacy of art in informing, delineating, circumscribing, and clarifying the seemingly insoluble problems of the postcolonial era. This is no small achievement. At the same time, the drama moves the audience to embrace in their hearts the truth that all disastrous political mistakes in the end are parsed into individual human pain and suffering. After all, it is women and men who endure tragedy, even as catastrophe engulfs a community.

CHARACTER DEVELOPMENT

Owen is the point-of-view character in the play—the one who expresses or maintains the playwright's position. He is a good son to his father and a good brother to his elder brother, Manus. He is an easygoing, intelligent, positive, well-dressed, urbane man. He would like to see prosperity and peace reign in the county of his birth, and he hopes that the English engineers and their major world language will be a force for good. When the English commanding officer gives information and instruction in English to the Irish-speaking populace, Owen mitigates the impact of the statements in translating. In the end, however, when catastrophe has struck, he sadly joins with his own people against the English. In the finale, one must choose a side.

Manus, handicapped from childhood, is an effective and caring teacher. He almost slavishly serves his autocratic father, living his forgiveness for the father who maimed him in a drunken act. He exists for the time he will marry Maire, never quite realizing, until it is too late, that she does not love him and will never be his bride. When he limps away from the burning town, his probable fate is imprisonment and execution at the hands of the revengeful English soldiers.

Hugh, the elderly, alcoholic schoolmaster, dreams of a new Athens as he teaches subjects of little practical value. However, his classical erudition gives him prestige and authority. He is one of the few in the town who knows English and who understands exactly what Captain Lancey is saying, but he takes no action to head off trouble. The passion for the classical past and his addiction to alcohol have debilitated him. Even when he was young and on the way with his friend Jimmy Jack to join the Irish rebel army revolting against the English in 1798, he and Jimmy Jack stopped at a tavern on the way to the field of battle and, after drinking, slinked back to Baile Beag while hundreds of other young Irish men fought and died for Ireland. Hugh is a man without a future: professionally and personally.

Maire is a young woman who enjoys the hedge school but would rather learn English than Latin. She, more than anyone else in the community, understands the practicality of learning a second language that is widely in use in the world rather than a language used only by scholars and churchmen. Maire is already considering emigration to America when the play opens. She falls in love with Yolland partly because she is enamored with his exotic Englishness, in the same way that he is fascinated by her exotic Irishness.

Lieutenant Yolland is a shy person, not very military in appearance, who became a soldier because he missed the ship that was supposed to take him to India to make his fortune. He enjoys his friendship with Owen, and he eventually gets the hang of doing the renaming with his Irish pal. Most of all, Yolland has quickly become a Hibernophile, loving the landscape, the sound of Irish, and most of all Maire, the beautiful young woman he meets in the hedge school. Not knowing the language or understanding the people, blinded by love, Yolland is blithely unaware of the suspicion of foreigners, especially the English military, that stirs some of the community of Baile Beag. Most dangerously, in his innocence he does not consider that many young men would resent the fact that one of their young women is being "stolen" by an outsider.

Sarah has long been considered a hopeless mute by the community, but she has been learning to speak under the patient tutelage of Manus, of whom she is very fond. When she discovers Maire and Yolland in a kiss, she blurts out the word "Manus," and the next thing the audience knows is that Yolland has disappeared. Sarah has used her newly acquired ability to communicate to inform on the couple, an action that leads to the destruction of her own community. Realizing this, when she is interrogated by the angry Lancey, the traumatized young woman loses the power of speech once more. The ability to communicate has proved too dangerous to her.

Jimmy Jack is a man in his sixties who comes to the classes because he enjoys reading and conversations in classical Greek and Latin, languages he is proficient in. He is filthy, and he never changes his clothes. His world is the ancient one, inhabited by heroes, gods, and goddesses, one of whom, Pallas Athene, he is preparing to marry. He, like his contemporary Hugh, also finds escape in drink.

Captain Lancey is a no-nonsense, middle-aged professional soldier and a cartographer. He has little understanding of the Irish people. He is not well educated, and he knows no Irish, nor is he interested in learning the language or the culture he is subverting by his work and even his presence in uniform. He will let nothing stand in the way of his successful completion of his mission. Ironically, he destroys a community he is in the process of renaming.

THEMES

Translations is a play about the problematizing of communication and the difficulties as well as the failures of translating not only between languages but more significantly between cultures. Even when people are speaking the same language, they still experience loss or confusion because communication is seldom if ever pure and because the very act of turning a thought into speech is an act of translation. There is always an interpreter on the other end.

The struggle between languages as the chief conveyors of culture is always a struggle for power. Thus, a major theme of the play is the limitations of investing in the politics of language controversy, such as the usefulness of Latin and Greek or the conflict between Irish and English. Yolland knows that even if he learns to speak Irish fluently, he will always be an outsider. Friel hints that the energy expended by the Irish on the famed "Irish eloquence" comes at the expense of material gains. It is fine to be a spiritual people, but great effort must be made in the temporal sphere so that a people can have better shelter than mud cabins and more food crops than the sometimes unreliable, blight-ridden potato and more industry beyond subsistence farming with the continual fear of crop failure and famine.

Anyway, a common language will not alone make a common people. Friel tries to deal with a perennial Irish question: Are the Irish culturally displaced in their own land? Or are they are at home in Irish English, having challenged the conqueror on the field of literature so that in modern times they have produced world-class poetry, fiction, and drama while winning four Nobel prizes for literature, awarded to William Butler Yeats, George Bernard Shaw, Samuel Beckett, and Seamus Heaney?

Another major theme in *Translations* is the failure of violence to solve colonial problems. This theme has long been on the author's mind, as warfare among the Irish Republican Army, Ulster paramilitary groups, the Ulster constabulary, and the British army has caused death and destruction on the island of Ireland throughout much of the twentieth century with an end not yet in sight.

NARRATIVE STYLE

The hedge school in *Translations* is located in a barn in Baile Beag, a small town in County Donegal, which will be renamed Ballybeg by the British. In fact, Ballybeg is a mythological name of a "historical" community created by Friel in which to set several of his plays, just as William Faulkner (1897–1962), the Nobel Prize–winning American novelist, created Yoknapatawpha County, Mississippi, in which to set many of his dark stories. Baile Beag means small town. *Translations*' town is a typical rural community whose old Irish traditions, values, and culture have been continually eroded from the late eighteenth century to the present.

Translations is divided into three acts, all of which are set in the realistically furbished hedge school barn. The barn evokes the poverty and isolation of the community. It still has its cow stalls. The students sit on wooden benches. Broken farm tools and jugs are scattered about. There is a pail of water at the door for washing.

Mapmaking, the work of the British Army Corps of Engineers, is a metaphor for the Anglicization of Ireland. The advantages for England are obvious. Changing the names of Irish places remakes the face of Ireland into its present look.

Class is defined by clothing. Manus's is shabby. Owen is dressed in the apparel of a Dublin gentleman of the time. Their father, Hugh, is also shabbily dressed, although he carries a walking stick that he imperiously hands to Manus on entering as if he were giving it to a footman. Captain Lancey and Lieutenant Yolland, of course, are wearing the uniforms of officers of the British army.

Friel uses several languages in *Translations:* primarily English, of course, but sometimes English represents Irish; sometimes characters are actually speaking Irish; Greek and Latin are also spoken in the play. Not surprisingly, language is the source of conflict.

Although Friel employs a simple conversational mode for his dialogue, *Translations* very much looks and feels like a history play to the audience. Hugh and Jack recall the rebellion of 1798. Contemporary historical references are many, such as the lack of confidence the townspeople have for the political leader Daniel O'Connell, whose program of accommodation to the British government in order to further nationalist and Catholic interests is disapproved of. The coming of the National Schools is looked on with distrust. Most of the people do not want their children to be taught in English because they fear the loss of Irish in the generations to come. When there is a sweet smell in the air, they speak of the potato blight that brings hunger, and the audience connects that with the knowledge that a dozen years later the greatest famine in Irish history will occur because of the failure of the potato crop. A million Irish will die of starvation or disease; another million will emigrate to North America, Canada, or England itself; and the Irish language will come close to disappearing on the island.

HISTORICAL CONTEXT

Translations is set in the summer of 1833 in a County Donegal hedge school for adults, originally an illegal school conducted in the Irish language, and run by priests and laypeople dedicated to preserving the Catholic religion and the old tongue of the people. The Penal Laws of the eighteenth century imposed on Catholic Ireland by the British government had resulted in the confiscation of nearly all remaining Catholic land, the disenfranchising of the Catholic inhabitants of Ireland, and the outlawing of the Catholic religion. Therefore, Catholic worship and education went underground, in this case into the thick hedges of the Irish countryside. But now the hedge schools are no longer hidden, and this one is in a disused barn.

Oddly, however, to a large extent it was pagan classics of ancient Greece and Rome that were taught in Irish. Thus, ironically, the curricula of both Irish and English schools in the late eighteenth and early nineteenth centuries were much the same. The time of the play, 1833, is one of transition. The British authorities are in the process of establishing National Schools where conditions will be better, instructors better trained, tuition free, and the language of instruction English. But the schools are also instruments of linguistic imperialism, for language is a cornerstone of a people's cultural identity. Many would argue that to supersede one language with another is to destroy the culture of the speakers of the former.

The British are also in the process of surveying the country so that ordnance maps can be drawn, roads can be built, and place-names will be both clarified and translated into English. Many Irish people resented the surveying of their country because they believed—correctly—that good roads made it easier to move troops and thus control the countryside.

In 1833, the urban centers of Ireland, especially Dublin, had more hope for the future despite the Act of Union in 1800, which had brought about the disbanding of the Protestant-only Irish Parliament in Dublin. After Catholic emancipation in 1829, brought about by the leadership of the brilliant Catholic lawyer Daniel O'Connell (1775–1847), Ireland sent Catholic as well as Protestant members to the British Parliament in Westminster. The Irish-speaking O'Connell next hoped to see Parliament repeal the Act of Union so that once more an Irish Parliament could sit in Dublin but this time with Catholic as well as Protestant legislators. Tragically for Ireland, that was not to be.

The people of the rural west of Ireland, Irish speakers, were suspicious not only of the intentions of the English but even of O'Connell when it came to the maintaining of their culture, especially their language.

SUGGESTED READINGS

Andrews, Elmer. *The Art of Brian Friel*. New York: St. Martin's, 1995.

Friel, Brian. *Translations*. London: Faber and Faber, 1995.

McGrath, F.C. *Brian Friel's (Post)Colonial Drama: Language, Illusion, and Politics*. Syracuse, N.Y.: Syracuse University Press, 1999.

O'Brien, George. *Brian Friel*. Boston: Twayne, 1989.

10

Caryl Churchill
Top Girls
1982

Caryl Churchill's plays are an especially good example of the new sensibilities in contemporary British drama. Her plays are mainstream, but they espouse such causes as feminism, gay rights, and tolerance and respect for people of color in Britain and elsewhere. Churchill's feminism is particularly British because she incorporates her ardent socialism in it. It is not about the bourgeois-style success of a few women in the "man's world." Those women too often pride themselves on being as good as men in their areas of enterprise while doing little for other women. Churchill would say, They are women, but they are not sisters. Her agenda calls for collective action by women to achieve equality and justice for all women. When first produced, *Top Girls* received instant celebrity. Subsequent productions in Great Britain, North America, and Ireland confirmed the play's status as a predictor of the working woman's dilemma for the years to come. *Top Girls* has proved to be intensely pleasurable for female audiences.

Churchill's plays often indict society for allowing the threat or use of violence on women's bodies to control them. Churchill is also well aware of the failure of Western society to recognize and use fully the different perspective that women contribute to political life.

Churchill's comedy is parodistic; it is expressed in witty dialogue, mischievous characterizations, and playful dramaturgy. Her plots are strong, and she is acutely aware of speech rhythms. Her main subjects are the plight of the powerless, the exploitation of women, and the dark, obsessive dreams that burden human beings.

BIOGRAPHICAL CONTEXT

Caryl Churchill is the best-known British woman dramatist. Her plays are performed all over the world. She was born in London in 1938. Her father was a political cartoonist, and her mother was a fashion model, minor film actress, and sometime secretary who had left school at the age of 14. The Churchill family emigrated to Canada in 1948, where Churchill was educated at the Trafalgar School in Montreal from 1948 to 1955. Returning to Britain in 1957, Churchill entered Lady Margaret Hall, one of Oxford's colleges for women. During that time, Churchill's early plays were produced by local and university companies. She received a bachelor of arts degree in English in 1960. The next year, she married David Harter, a lawyer. The couple has three sons.

During the remainder of the 1960s, Churchill was busy caring for her family. She did, however, write radio and television plays. These plays mirrored the homebound woman's depression. In 1974, Churchill became the first female writer-in-residence at the Royal Court Theatre. Churchill now has written more than 15 performed stage plays, and she has won many playwriting awards, including the Olivier Award in 1987.

In *Owners* (1972), Churchill's first professionally produced play, a group of people become involved in a series of hapless relationships. The play is about motherhood, social control, ownership, and money in a macabre plot in which a mother offers her baby in exchange for a place to live. *Light Shining in Buckinghamshire* (1976) discusses the libertarian ideas and values in seventeenth-century England that led to utopianism, while impoverished women are publicly stripped to the waist and flogged for being contrary or just unforgivably poor and middle-class women terrorized and conditioned to feel self-hatred. Even in church, a woman is beaten for trying to speak. It is on the woman's body that church and state inscribe their power.

Vinegar Tom (1976) is about witch hunts in the seventeenth century when the profession of medicine, full of misogyny and run by men of course, clashed with midwifery, persecuting the women who had been delivering babies safely for generations. When women cannot be controlled and "kept in their place," they are subject to imprisonment, torture, and hanging as witches. Religious and temporal authority combine to persecute the most vulnerable members of society: poor, old, or unmarried women.

Cloud Nine (1979) is one of Churchill's finest dramatic achievements. Set in Victorian Africa and modern London, it is a hilariously outrageous farce that links British imperialism with racism and sexual oppression while it contrasts the sexual hypocrisy of British colonialism in the Victorian age with the sexual freedom in contemporary Britain.

Top Girls (1982) features an unmarried woman executive who sacrifices the future of her daughter for her career and lives to regret it. *Fen* (1983) is about the hard life of English female agricultural workers. *Softcops* (1984), a response to the French philosopher Michel Foucault's *Discipline and Punishment* (1977), is an all-male play set in nineteenth-century France that discusses the developing theories and institutions of discipline and punishment as well as the interrelationship of criminals and cops as they subvert authority.

Written like a Restoration satire, *Serious Money* (1986), an international success, is about the City of London, Britain's Wall Street, in the greedy 1980s. The stock market is, of course, the epitome of capitalism and the most worthy of targets for Churchill's socialism. Stock prices are illegally manipulated, a brokerage collapses, Third World dictators misappropriate money directed toward their people, and the profit motive rules supreme. Morality is only a public relations ploy. Even blatant murder can be turned into a verdict of suicide if enough money is involved. For Churchill, a life of merely making money is hardly worth living.

A Mouthful of Birds (1987) presents a picture of women in the thrall of pleasure and violence, often related and mutually satisfying. *Mad Forest: A Play for Romania* (1990) is one of the first dramas on the demise of communism in 1989. It tells the people's story of the fall of the iron-fisted despot Nicolae Ceausescu. *The Skriker* (1994) is a visionary exploration of urban life in which a female goblin, able to change form at will, stalks two young women to London. The play incorporates music to create an aura of fantastical primitivism. In *Far Away* (2000), a Pinter-like drama, Britain is sinking into authoritarian barbarism, the nation's future is apocalyptic, and its demise is not far away. *A Number* (2004) is one of the first plays about genetic engineering and its effect on contemporary society.

PLOT DEVELOPMENT

Top Girls, an all-woman play, has one of the most brilliant openings in the entire history of modern British drama. It begins with a sparkling celebration of the achievement of significant women in history or legend. In the long first act, all the women are top girls in one way or another. The fantastical scene is self-contained. Only Marlene, who is hosting the restaurant party to celebrate her promotion to managing director of the Top Girls Employment Agency, connects to the rest of the play, which is naturalistic. But the limitations of unique individual achievement by women is purposely deconstructed by Churchill. Individual achievement, fame, or notoriety of women is of little ultimate significance if the societies they lived in were or are so restricted by patriarchy that only a few exceptional women could or can squeeze through gender barriers. Often even successful women find themselves cruelly punished for daring to be outstanding.

Marlene's guests at her mythic celebration are Isabella Bird, a nineteenth-century Scot who traveled extensively around the world from the age of 40 to 70; Lady Nijo, a thirteenth-century Japanese royal courtesan and later a Buddhist nun; Dull Gret, a subject in a Brueghel painting in which a woman in armor leads a crowd of other women charging through hell to fight the devils; Pope Joan, who, disguised as a man, is thought to have been the pope from A.D. 854 to 856; and Patient Griselda, the obedient wife whose parable-like story is told in "The Clerk's Tale" in Chaucer's *The Canterbury Tales*. These women share with each other the pain they had in sacrificing their personal lives in order to obtain a significant place in an unforgiving patriarchal society. They also suffered in various ways for defying male dominance and societal expectation that they should aggrandize men. It is not surprising that the act ends in drunken disorder.

The subsequent acts are set in two locales. One is Marlene's employment office, where she has come to be "top girl," having competed with a male colleague, Howard, for the position. When his desperate wife pleads for Marlene to pass on the position because Howard's ego has been damaged by being bested by a woman and because he has a family to support, Marlene refused, of course. The other is the East Anglia home of her slatternly, working-class older sister, Joyce, and her "daughter," the psychologically underdeveloped and perhaps slightly retarded Angie, who near the end of the play is revealed to be Marlene's illegitimate child.

Joyce has not had the opportunities that Marlene has had, and she is bitter. She realizes that Marlene despises their impoverished origins and has done everything possible to conceal them. It seems clear that Angie will not have any success in life but will wind up like the woman she thinks is her mother: locked into a bleak, working-class life. The implied sociological message of the play is that opportunity for women must transcend class barriers that exist in contemporary Britain.

At the end of the play, Angie, who has long been suspicious that her "mother" is really her aunt, wakes up from a bad dream and mistakes "Aunt" Marlene for her "mother" Joyce. Angie would like to live with Marlene and grow up like Marlene, but her future will be Joyce's, not Marlene's, no matter what the latter will do for her. Marlene sacrificed Angie in order to have her "single" and mobile career. Her guilt is palpable. Clearly, no woman should have to make that decision.

CHARACTER DEVELOPMENT

Marlene stands for the ruthless, selfish, self-promoting stereotype of the Thatcherite Conservatives running Britain in the 1980s. The audience's admiration for her success in a man's world—especially in the spectacular act 1—is tempered by her neglect of her daughter and exploitation of her sister, her lack of sympathy for the wife of her competitor (the woman whose life has been damaged as much as her husband's has), and the fact that she is ashamed of her origins. She has cast her lot with the Reagan admirers in Britain who used his anticommunism as an excuse for embracing the cult of the individual and the abrogating of government responsibility for the commonweal.

Joyce is an all-suffering woman who has had a miserable marriage, and who had her own fetus aborted because she could not take care of an additional child when she had accepted responsibility for raising Angie as her own daughter. Joyce has earned a meager living for Angie and herself by doing menial jobs. Marlene has neglected to visit and help financially.

Angie is a pathetic 16-year-old whose only friend is a bright 12-year-old. She acts as if she is slightly retarded. She has little affection for Joyce, and when she visits Marlene's office in London, she makes it clear that she would prefer to live with her "aunt." She has enough intelligence to see that Joyce's life and Marlene's life are worlds apart, and she much prefers Marlene's. However, it is perfectly clear to Marlene, Joyce, and the audience that Angie will never rise out of what Marx called the "lumpen proletariat." She will never work at any but menial jobs, and witnessing Marlene's privileged middle-class existence is almost cruel. Her fate is sealed by her slow development and by the class into which she was delivered by Marlene: the lack of education and the general indifference of the capitalist society whose precepts her natural mother fervently embraces. Poor Angie represents all the abandoned and damaged children in a capitalistic world.

THEMES

As a social comedy, *Top Girls* explores the nature of success for women in the contemporary world, one still run by men, most of whom expect the successful woman to follow a male model in economic, social, professional, and personal ways. Churchill implies that a British woman's life can never be happy because she is either trapped by the wife/mother role or forced to repress her natural desire to give birth to and nurture a child in order to be free enough to fulfill her leadership potential and succeed in a career. No woman "can have it all."

Although Churchill challenges contemporary conventions in regard to gender roles and she is concerned that women are forced to embrace a capitalist work ethic at the expense of family and a commitment to sisterhood in order to gain a degree of status in the business world, she is not advocating the disengagement of women or the devaluing of family life. Feminism must not exclude marriage and motherhood. Churchill's attack on the cult of the individual, in which any humane value is expendable in the race for personal power and money, really applies to men as well as women. Men too fall into the money trap and struggle to survive in the zero-sum game of modern business.

Since the socioeconomic context shapes human relations, *Top Girls* ultimately asks society if the career woman, especially the exceptional one, must deny maternal and compassionate qualities in order to survive—let alone succeed—in the viciously competitive business world.

NARRATIVE STYLE

Churchill has a fine ear for everyday dialogue. Most of the speeches in *Top Girls* are under five lines, and the majority are one line or partial utterances. The effect is a fast-moving conversational style.

The author uses the two mature women in the play, Marlene and Joyce, to represent the opposite sides of the political debate in 1980s Britain. That debate was a mask for the class warfare that was first presented on stage with Osborne's *Look Back in Anger.* Joyce stands for the old egalitarian socialist position, one requiring heavy taxation of the wealthier classes to support the underprivileged and the indigent. Joyce argues for equality of opportunity. She hates those upwardly mobile Britons who despise the poor and believe, in a false Darwinian sense, that they were born superior to the lazy, heavy-drinking, promiscuous members of the "sometimes" working class. Joyce believes, naively, that the future will bring the rise of the working class and the stripping of privilege from the wealthy.

HISTORICAL CONTEXT

The Marriage Reform Act of 1969 and the international women's movement that had come into existence in the early 1970s resulted, in Britain, in a massive explosion of women's theater. Although militants in the movement argued against canon formation because such formations historically had been patriarchally created and enforced—to the exclusion of female writers, of course—it quickly became apparent that some female playwrights were achieving outstanding recognition in critical and academic circles, and thus the formation of a feminist canon was inevitable, irresistible, and indeed practical. Consequently, Caryl Churchill, along with Pam Gems and Sarah Daniels, became a central figure in the creation of a new British political drama based on the radical feminist movement.

British publishers like Methuen began to initiate play series by women writers. The improved social and economic condition of women gave them power in the British theater world and elsewhere. Women's drama production companies like the Women's Theatre Group, The Sphinx, Monstrous Regiment, and Clean Break flourished, and the more traditional venues like the Royal Court Theatre and the Royal Shakespeare Company initially and then the Old Vic and the National Theatre began to feature the work of female dramatists.

Meanwhile, British artists on the Left took aim at the new conservatism in politics, symbolized by Prime Minister Margaret Thatcher, a "top girl" indeed, who reduced or eliminated many of the social programs of the previous Labour government. Like Brecht and Harold Pinter—the British contemporary playwrights with whom she has most in common—Churchill uses the stage as a pulpit to promote her liberal social views and her fear of the possibility of right-wing entrepreneurial ardor becoming totalitarianism in her country, America, and perhaps the entire Western world.

SUGGESTED READINGS

Churchill, Caryl. *Top Girls*. London: Methuen, 1990.
Randall, Phyllis R., ed. *Caryl Churchill: A Casebook*. New York: Garland, 1989.

Selected Bibliography

Aston, Elaine, and Janelle Reinelt, eds. *The Cambridge Companion to Modern British Women Playwrights*. Cambridge: Cambridge University Press, 2000.

Bull, John. *New British Political Dramatists*. New York: Grove, 1983; London: Macmillan, 1984.

Corrigan, Robert W. *The Theatre in Search of a Fix*. New York: Dell, 1973.

Elsom, John. *Post-War British Theatre*. London: Routledge and Kegan Paul, 1976.

Etherton, Michael. *Contemporary Irish Dramatists*. London: Macmillan, 1989.

Fitz-Simon, Christopher. *The Irish Theatre*. London: Thames and Hudson, 1983.

Grene, Nicholas. *The Politics of Irish Drama: Plays Context from Boucicault to Friel*. Cambridge: Cambridge University Press, 1999.

Hayman, Ronald. *British Theatre since 1955*. Oxford: Oxford University Press, 1979.

Houghton, Norris. *The Exploding Stage: An Introduction to Twentieth-Century Drama*. New York: Dell, 1971.

Innes, Christopher. *Modern British Drama: The Twentieth Century*. Cambridge: Cambridge University Press, 2002.

Maxwell, D. E. S. *A Critical History of Modern Irish Drama*. Cambridge: Cambridge University Press, 1984.

Murray, Christopher. *Twentieth Century Irish Drama: A Mirror Up to Nation*. Manchester: Manchester University Press, 1997.

Peacock, D. Keith. *Radical Stages: Alternate History in Modern British Drama*. New York: Greenwood, 1991.

Raby, David Ian. *British and Irish Political Drama in the Twentieth Century: Implicating the Audience*. New York: St. Martin's, 1986.

Rebellato, Dan. *1956 and All That: The Making of Modern British Drama*. London: Routledge, 1999.

Roche, Anthony. *Contemporary Irish Drama: From Beckett to McGuinness*. Dublin: Gill and Macmillan, 1994.

Rusinko, Susan. *British Drama 1950 to the Present: A Critical History*. Boston: Twayne, 1989.

Shellard, Dominic. *British Theatre since the War*. New Haven, Conn.: Yale University Press, 1999.

Taylor, John Russell. *Anger and After*. Rev. ed. Harmondsworth: Penguin, 1963.

Wandor, Michelene. *Post War British Drama: Looking Back in Gender*. London: Routledge, 2001.

Index

About the Author

SANFORD STERNLICHT is Professor of English at Syracuse University. He has published several books of poetry, and his scholarly studies include *A Reader's Guide to Modern Irish Drama* (1998), *Chaim Potok: A Critical Companion* (Greenwood, 2000), and *Student Companion to Elie Wiesel* (Greenwood, 2003)

DATE DUE
